KU-168-981

INSIGHT **POCKET GUIDE**

CORFU

Discovery
CHANNEL

APA PUBLICATIONS
Part of the Langenscheidt Publishing Group

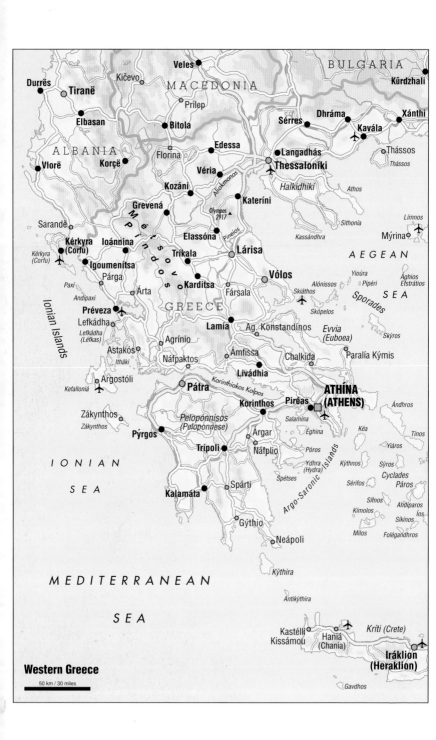

Western Greece

50 km / 30 miles

introduction

Welcome

The aim of this book is to help visitors get the most out of Corfu during a short stay of a week or two, and to this end Insight's main expert on Greece and its islands, Elizabeth Boleman-Herring, has created a series of carefully crafted itineraries. The tours link the island's highlights, but also explore many delightful corners that only someone intimately acquainted with Corfu is likely to know. They take in monasteries, churches, markets, offshore islets, secluded bays and even alternative health centres.

Supporting the itineraries are sections on history and culture, shopping, eating out and nightlife, plus a detailed practical information section, which includes a list of hand-picked hotels and pensions.

Elizabeth Boleman-Herring first went to Corfu, or Kérkyra, as the Greeks call it, in 1961. She says of that first visit, 'My mother was reading to me from a first edition of Gerald Durrell's hysterical account of his Corfiot childhood, and my family all swam endlessly in the incredible turquoise sea off the east coast, giggling over passages from *My Family and Other Animals*. Someone bought me my first bikini – blue and white polka dots – in Kérkyra (Corfu Town), but I promptly lost the top half in the sea, and so became an early advocate of Hellenic toplessness. I remember crying bitterly when compelled to return to school in Athens.'

Boleman-Herring has often returned to that azure Ionian Sea, forging strong bonds on neighbouring Kefalloniá and Itháki. But her true favourites among the Ionians are Corfu, the tiny Dhiapóndia islets which are part and parcel of Kérkyra, and nearby Paxí – pristine, sophisticated – and also revisited in this guide.

6 contents

HISTORY AND CULTURE

Corfu was coveted by many nations, and won by a few. The Romans, Byzantines, Venetians, French and British played a part in the shaping of the island, but it was one man who left the most constant legacy – St Spýridhon **11**

ITINERARIES

These 17 itineraries not only show you the best of the island, but also draw you into the culture and every-day life of the Corfiots.

1 **The Historic Centre** is a tour of Kérkyra, including the *Archaeological Museum*, the *Ancient Fortress*, the *Museum of Asian Art* and the *Church of the Miracleworking St Spýridhon*..**23**

2 **Palace and New Fortress** completes the tour of Kérkyra's historic centre. It includes the *Municipal Gallery*, the *Byzantine Museum* and also the *Church of the Virgin Panagía* and the *New Fortress* **29**

3 **The Ahíllion and Dhassiá** comprises a tour of the Empress Elisabeth's residence on Corfu and a visit to the seaside resort of *Dhassiá* **32**

4 **Kanóni and Mount Pandokrátor** explores the little 'suburb' of *Kanóni* and the island of *Pondikoníssi*, with a late afternoon trip up to *Mount Pandokrátor* **35**

5 **The Campiello Quarter** is a stroll around Venetian and medieval Kérkyra, taking in the *Cathedral*, some churches and a section of the *Venetian Walls* **39**

6 **By Hydrofoil to Paxí** explores a beautiful, unspoilt island with pretty towns and wonderful beaches.........**42**

7 **Ághios Stéfanos Sinión and Agní** takes you to two picturesque beach hamlets that are noted for their gastronomic delights..**44**

8 **By Caïque to Eríkoussa Islet** offers a boat trip from the resort of *Sidhári* to the peaceful and beautiful Diapóndhian islet of *Eríkoussa* **45**

9 **Alonáki Bay and the South** meanders down the west coast, via the fortress of *Gardhíki,* en route to beaches and a birdwatchers' paradise, *Lake Korissíon* **48**

10 **Alternative Corfu** gives you a number of options for indulging yourself and getting to know some real Corfiots in the process **50**

11 *Au Naturel* **at Myrtiótissa Beach** lets you get an all-over tan and do some skinny-dipping at Corfu's only (unofficial) nudist beach. **52**

12   Angelókastro and Paleokastrítsa includes the 12th-century *Angelókastro,* perched high above the sea, and the lovely resort town of *Paleokastrítsa,* with its 13th-century *Monastery of the Holy Virgin* **54**

13   Folklore Heritage of Corfu explores the life of old Corfu at the *folklore museum* in *Sinarádhes* then spends the evening at a luxury hotel to enjoy a display of authentic Greek dancing **56**

14   Sunday in Kérkyra begins with a service at *Holy Trinity Anglican Church,* before touring the fascinating *British Cemetery,* seeing a movie at the open-air cinema and ending the evening at the New Fortress's *Morrison Café* **58**

15   Western Beaches and Sport offers a round of golf, a walk along the *Corfu Trail,* and/or watersports, or simply lazing on a beautiful beach **61**

16   The Wild, Woolly East takes you to the busy holiday resorts of the east coast, including *Benítses* and *Kávos,* with a side trip to peaceful, pastoral *Hlómós* up in the hills of the hinterland **63**

17   Northeast Coast by Caïque takes to the sea in a traditional Greek fishing caïque to explore the stunning, secluded beaches and coves of the northeast coast, with a stop at Lawrence Durrell's *White House;* there are also details of scuba diving trips **65**

LEISURE ACTIVITIES

What to buy, where to eat, and where to go **69–79**

CALENDAR OF EVENTS

A list of the main events, festivals and celebrations on the island **80–81**

PRACTICAL INFORMATION

All the background information you are likely to need for your stay, with a list of hand-picked hotels **83–96**

MAPS

Western Greece	4	*Eastern Corfu*	36
Corfu	18–19	*Paxí and Andípaxi*	43
Corfu Town	20–21	*Northern Corfu*	46
Central Corfu	33	*Southern Corfu*	49

CREDITS AND INDEX

pages **99–104**

Pages 2–3: the beach at Sidhári
Pages 8–9: icons on display at the Angelókastro

History
&Culture

I f you were paying attention back in school when you first read Homer, you have already 'visited' Corfu, in the company of the wily Odysseus. Near the end of his storm-tossed wanderings, and harried until the last instant by the wrathful sea-god Poseidon, Odysseus washed up on the shores of Scheria, land of the seafaring Phaiakians – they of the great rudderless ships – and was rescued by the daughter of King Alkinoös, the tall and beautiful Nausikaa, who was playing ball with her maids on an exquisite beach.

Nausikaa's incomparable beach was, we conjecture, that of present-day Paleokastrítsa, still a kind of heaven on earth with azure waters, intimate coves, dramatic and verdant promontories – and still populated by beautiful young people. Homer describes it all lingeringly in Books V and VI of the *Odyssey*, and it is not hard to believe that it was on Corfu that Odysseus finally found a happy respite from his long ordeal.

The image of the rudderless ship of the Phaiakian seamen is still very much in evidence on Corfu – on buildings and monuments, and used as a logo for everything from Corfiot travel agencies to sailing clubs. Like all large, fertile islands, Corfu was principally settled and pillaged by great powers with vast fleets. But it wasn't so at the very beginning.

On Foot and by Sea They Came

The very earliest visitors, Stone-Age hunter-gatherers, strolled across from Epirus during the last great Ice Age, which began some 70,000 years ago, but by 10,000 years ago the ice had melted, the Mediterranean had risen, and later visitors would have to come by boat. And come they did.

The ancient Egyptians were among the earliest visitors, and *papyrelles*, boats made of papyrus (bulrushes) of the type used by Nile Delta mariners, have been found on Corfu's west coast. Another legacy of the Egyptians are the papyrus plants which still flourish here today. Where mariners dared, colonisers were sure to follow. In about 750BC, the Eretrians – from Euboea, north of Athens – colonised Corfu en route to Italy, defeating the first documented inhabitants of the island, the Liburnians.

The Eretrians were followed by the Corinthians in 734BC, and it was they who first left substantial evidence of their sojourn: city walls around their ancient town of Corcyra, located near the present day Mon Repos; kilns for firing their distinctive ceramics; and grand structures, such as the Temple of Artemis. But there were also important, intangible contributions by Corinth: parliamentary government and the introduction of mainland (Greek) religious beliefs.

Not much remains of Corinth's great monuments – there have been too many other movers and shakers,

Left: Odysseus and Nausikaa depicted by Allesandro Allori
Right: Homer, author of the *Odyssey*

plunderers and builders, who carted off the ancient stones for use in their own bastions and mansions. It wasn't long before Corcyra rose up against its colonial master and sought independence. In 660BC, history's first ever recorded naval battle took place between Corcyra and Corinth, though history failed to record who won. Skirmishes between the two great naval powers continued, with the last great conflagration, waged near the islets of Sybota in 433BC, causing the great Peloponnesian War (431–404BC).

They Came, They Saw, They Conquered

Civil war on Corcyra followed, between the island's aristocrats (favouring Corinth and Sparta) and its democrats (siding with Athens). After much bloodshed, Corcyra fell to the Lacedaemonian general, Kleonymos, in 303BC; then, in 301BC, to Agathokles, Tyrant of Syracuse, and to Ptolemy in 284BC. A pattern was emerging in this corner of the Ionian Sea: the rich pearl that was Corfu – rich for strategic purposes as well as for its natural resources – would be snatched by successive waves of invaders. Corfiot history, from the 3rd century BC on, may be seen as a revolving door of European predation, though those who came to plunder invariably left something of value in their wake.

Distinguishing between pirates and protectors must have proved difficult for the Corfiots, since a veritable parade of both were subsequently to descend upon the island. A glance at a map hints at the reason, and shows a remarkable geographic similarity to the 'great boot' of Italy – Corfu resembles a little boot, its ankle symbolically flexed back to kick something away. The ancients saw the island as a harp or scythe shape, and named it accordingly, but the modern name comes from the Greek word *korifón*, after the pair of summits now crowned by the Old and New Fortresses.

The Romans, provoked beyond endurance by attacks on their mariners by Illyrian pirates, declared war on them in around 229BC. The Illyrians,

Above: the great Peloponnesian War

in turn, laid siege to Corfu, but the island was immediately liberated by Caius Fulvius, and placed itself willingly under the protection of its powerful neighbour. The Romans would stay on for the next five centuries, and some illustrious Italians visited Corcyra: Cicero and Cato; Marc Antony and Octavia; Agrippina and her children, Julia and Caligula.

In AD40 two disciples of St Paul, saints Jason and Sosipater, brought Christianity to Corfu and established the island's first church, St Stephen's – which explains the plethora of modern place names reading Ághios or San (Saint) Stefanos around the island.

Following the splitting of the Roman Empire by Diocletian late in the 3rd century into western and eastern portions – the latter to become Byzantium – Corfu's regime changed. It was to remain, on and off, a possession of Byzantium until 1204, which saw the fall of Constantinople. This great capital was the cradle of Orthodoxy, and the fall of 'The City' is still considered by Greeks to be, after the Crucifixion, the darkest day in history. Life between the 4th and 13th centuries was – here as in most of Europe – nasty, brutal and short, with a series of Pythonesque barbarians storming the twin peaks. The Vandals sacked the island in 455, followed by the Goths in 550; the Saracens attacked repeatedly between the 7th and 11th centuries. In 1081 the island was taken by the Normans, under Robert Guiscard; they were subsequently defeated by the Venetians, but then returned under Bohemond, Robert's son, only to be defeated by the Byzantines… to return again under Robert's nephew, Roger II of Sicily! No wonder the islanders finally took to the heights of the town and erected strong walls.

For three weeks during 1203, the bays were filled with the vast fleet of the Fourth Crusade, which weighed anchor here on its way to sack Constantinople. It was an awesome display, but for once the fleet had their sights on a richer trophy than the little Ionian isle.

The Most Serene Republic

Much of what we regard today as 'Corfiot' – the Old and New Fortresses, the narrow streets *(kantoúnia)* and their elegant residences, the lovely cobbled squares and Italianate churches, the Roman Catholic cathedral, the elaborately decorated government buildings – is, in fact, Venetian.

Of all the conquerors and administrators, pirates and protectors that Corfu has seen, none left such an impression as The Most Serene Republic. The Venetians, who occupied Corfu for a mere 400 years (compared with the millennium of Byzantine and Frankish domination), left a distinctive mark on the island's skyline, its social organisation, its forms of cultural expression – even its cuisine – that remains to this day. One may still sit on the Spianádha, a lovely town green originally cleared to give a free field for Venetian artillery, dining on Venetian delicacies in the company of a direct descendant of someone listed among the 'first families' in the Venetian *Libro d'Oro* and

Right: the head of Marc Antony, a Roman visitor to Corfu

be serenaded by musicians singing Venetian *Kandádhes*. It is as though the Serenissima (the 'Most Serene' republic) has only recently – and temporarily – departed.

Venetians came to Corfu to govern and plant olive trees, not simply to plunder, and they built fortresses to repel the most determined of foes. There were, of course, Byzantine and Angevin forts on Corfu before the Venetians, but these were built to safeguard garrisons, rather than to protect the people. Venice strove to fortify all of Corfu, assigning its military architects to the construction of the defences, with a network of tunnels to maintain communications in time of siege.

The Venetians were invitees, not conquerors – their assistance had been sought to ward off the attentions of the ruler of Padua in 1386. In 1387 a treaty that was to hold for the next 410 years formalised relations between the Doge and Corfu's nobility. Venice was to defend Corfu, but was barred from intervening in its feudal affairs, where the rich remained aloof and powerful, the poor went hungry and served the rich, and a middle class did not exist at all until after the 17th century.

In addition to all the civic building, the Venetians also brought organised Roman Catholicism to Corfu, ushering in a period of religious tension that was compounded by their motto, 'We are first Venetians, and then Christians'. Many Corfiots felt themselves to be first Greek Orthodox, second Christians, and Corfiots subservient to Venice as a distant third.

Barbarians at the Gate

All, however, were united in supporting the motto: 'First: NOT DEAD at the hands of the Genoese or, heaven forbid, the Ottoman Turks.' Any threat to Venetian peace over the next four centuries came primarily from without, not within. The Genoese spearheaded the agression, first in 1403 with their failed attempt to storm Angelókastro – visitors to this remarkable castle on the west coast will wonder why any besieger would even try.

The Ottoman Turks were a more formidable foe than Genoa, laying siege to the island five times between 1430 and 1716, but still Corfu was spared the fate of most of the rest of Greece and never fell beneath the Ottoman yoke – due entirely to the fortifications erected by Venice. The final siege, mounted early in the 18th century, was repulsed due to the heroic efforts of Saxon Field-Marshal Johann Matthias von der Schulenburg, aided by the timely arrival of Maltese Knights of St John, along with reinforcements from Spain, Genoa and Venice itself. The siege and the battles waged during the first half of 1716 are the stuff of legend, and the victory was credited to the

Above: Coptic angel, a sign of eastern influence

other-worldly intervention of the island's patron saint, Spyrídhon, whereupon it was decreed that there would be an annual procession on 11 August to honour the saint. On a more terrestrial level, a statue of Schulenburg, now outside the entrance to the Old Fortress, was commissioned, and Vivaldi composed a commemorative oratorio.

French and British Intervention

Delivered from the east, and, as it were, the past, Corfu now entered the modern age, and yet foreign occupiers were still to arrive, in the form of the revolutionary French. They came in peace in 1797 and stayed on to liberate the serfs, establish free trade and shock the locals with their atheism.

Defeated by a Russo-Turkish fleet in 1799, the French departed, and in 1800 the Ionian islands finally achieved a sort of independent nationhood as the Septinsular State. John Kapodhistrias, as first Minister of the Interior, reformed the island's fiscal system and, in so doing, dealt a death blow to the long-entrenched Corfiot aristocracy. Between 1804 and 1807, Corfu, for the first time in its long history, began to attract some prosperity.

But it was not to last. In August 1807, the imperial French annexed the Ionians and held them until April 1814, when, following Napoleon's defeat, the British peacefully occupied Corfu. A year later they were ceded all of the Ionians. The first British High Commissioner, Thomas Maitland, was instrumental in establishing a constitution, Greek Orthodoxy was declared the state religion and Greek the official language – something of a problem for Kérkyra's large, Italian-speaking, Jewish and aristocratic communities.

The British left a lasting legacy – monuments, fortifications, public works. Although the Ionian Greeks' desire for union *(énosis)* with Greece became vociferous, the transition, when it came, was peaceful. Given leave to select the successor to the deposed German King Otto of the Greeks, the British chose Crown Prince George Glücksburg of Denmark. As a condition of acceding the Greek throne, George I (as he would become) demanded that Britain cede the Ionian islands to his kingdom, and so on 16 May 1864, the act of termination of the 'British protection' was signed.

Today, though cricket is still played by Corfiots, Corfu is quintessentially Greek. It is now part of a regional governmental unit that votes Socialist and depends on tourism.

But more conservative culturally, Corfiots cling to their Christian faith and traditional Greek mores: the family is all, and hard work, to provide for the next generation's education and improvement, is axiomatic. Tending the millions of olive trees that comprise one of Venice's greatest living legacies to Corfu, Greece and Europe, and serving the new invaders of summer are the islanders' two primary objectives. But everyone on Corfu can always make time for 'philharmonic society' (read marching brass band) practice, and for honouring St Spyrídhon.

Right: Corfu became part of Napoleon's empire

history/culture

St Spýridhon, the Spirit of Corfu

Speaking of Corfu and its patron saint, Lawrence Durrell wrote: 'The island is really the Saint: and the Saint is the island.' For in Greece, each place has its own reverend patron and so does each individual Greek – a saint whose name he bears and whose annual name day he celebrates. In the case of a huge number of Corfiots, this is St Spýridhon.

The saint is Corfu's most revered and influential resident, his mummy encased in a silver reliquary and enthroned like royalty in the red-domed church that bears his name. The faithful who bend to kiss his tiny slippers would never countenance the fact that Spýridhon was not always a saint, nor ever, indeed, a Corfiot. Born in the middle of the 4th century AD, he became a shepherd in the mountains of Cyprus, but though poor and uneducated he attained a reputation for piety, self-sacrifice and wisdom. He married, but his beloved wife died giving birth to his only child, Irini. When she came of age she was made a nun, and her father retired into a monastery.

Eventually, he was named Bishop of Trimithion, and accounts of his Solomon-like wisdom began to be recorded, mixing legend and fact. There are stories of miracles performed during his lifetime, but none compares with those the saint accomplished after his death in AD350. In life, Spýridhon may have confined himself to meting out individual justice and homely logic; in death he would rout Turk, plague and famine.

Spýridhon's body was taken to Constantinople during the 7th century but by the mid-15th century that city was no longer safe for Christians, alive or dead, and George Kaloheiritis, the priest in whose church St Spýridhon reposed, decided to move his holy charge. He set out across what is now northern Greece and eventually came to Corfu, where he married and produced three sons, to whom he willed the holy relics. His son, Phillip, also a priest, considered moving Spýridhon to Venice, but the Corfiots' tearful entreaties stopped him.

The Church of the Miracleworking St Spýridhon in Kérkyra is filled with votive offerings. There are four great miracles performed by the saint on behalf of his island that are commemorated by processing his relics through the town. The first is commemorated on Easter Saturday, celebrating St Spýridhon's deliverance of the island from famine; the Palm Sunday procession recalls Corfu's salvation from plague in 1629; the first Sunday in November marks its deliverance from cholera in 1673. The last great miracle was performed on 24 June 1716, when St Spýridhon is said to have appeared to the Ottoman army, holding a 'sword flashing lightning and furiously pursuing them'. The Ottomans fled, and the fourth annual procession of the saint was instituted on 11 August.

For the people of Corfu, the saint is a touchstone and talisman. The finest greeting and farewell in Corfu is: *'O Ághios Spyrídonas mazí sou'* – 'May St Spýridhon be with you'.

Left: candles to St Spýridhon

HISTORY HIGHLIGHTS

70,000–40,000BC Prehistoric inhabitation of the island.

750BC Eretrians, Greeks from Euboea, subdue Illyrian Liburnians, Corfu's first documented residents.

734BC Led by Chersicrates, Corinthians colonise Corcyra, at Kanóni.

660BC First naval battle in history fought between Corinth and Corcyra.

433BC Battle between Corinth and Corcyra leads to Peloponnesian War.

427–425BC Corcyran civil war between aristocrats and democrats.

229BC Illyrians mount siege of Corcyra; Romans seize power.

AD37–41 Jason, Bishop of Tarsus, and Sosipater, the Bishop of Ikonium, disciples of St Paul, bring Christianity to Corcyra.

325 Spýridhon, Bishop of Trimithion, Cyprus, participates in First Ecumenical Synod of Nicaea. He is later canonised.

Late 3rd century AD Emperor Diocletian divides Roman Empire into western and eastern halves; Corcyra becomes part of the Eastern Roman, later Byzantine Empire.

455 Vandals sack Corcyra.

550 Goths sack Corcyra.

1081 Normans, under Robert Guiscard, seize island; subsequent Imperial Byzantine and Venetian incursions.

1191 Final expulsion of Normans by Byzantines.

1203 Fourth Crusade stops off at Corfu en route to Constantinople

1204 Constantinople falls to Latin Catholics.

1205 Venetians seize Corfu, dividing it, in 1207, among 10 feudal lords of Venice.

1267 According to the Treaty of Viterbo, the Angevins, of Naples, are ceded Corfu, and exploit its vineyards, olives and salt pans.

1267–1386 During Angevin rule, Corfu's Jewish community burgeons.

1386 Venice, invited by the Corfiots, takes possession of the island on 28 May. Venetian domination extends until 1797, sparing Corfu the ravages of Ottoman Turkish rule.

1493 New wave of Jews arrive, fleeing the Inquisition in Spain.

1537 First great Turkish siege of Corfu; countryside sacked and islanders carried off as slaves.

1576–88 Venice erects great city walls and fortresses at Kérkyra.

1571 Second Ottoman siege.

1716 Great Ottoman siege repulsed by Corfiots, Venetians and allies, under Saxon Field-Marshal Johann Matthias von der Schulenburg; victory attributed to St Spýridhon's intervention.

1722–8 Kérkyra is further fortified.

1797–9 Following Napoleon's defeat of Venice, Ionian islands are ceded to the French Republic.

1799 Russians and Turks defeat French and seize island.

1800–7 The semi-independent Septinsular state established by Russia and Turkey, under President Count Spýridhon-George Theotokis.

1807–14 Russians cede Ionians to the Imperial French.

1815 With the Treaty of Paris, the Ionians fall under British Protection.

1823 Ionian Academy, first modern Greek university, founded.

1823 John Kapodistrias elected first president of Independent Greece.

1864 King George of Greece arrives on 21 May; Protectorate ends.

1941 Corfu surrenders to Italy.

1943 Nazis occupy the island, execute Italian officers, and remove Jews to Germany for extermination.

1944 Germans depart after blowing up harbour installations.

1951 Club Mediterranée opens in Ípsos.

1994 Corfu is the site of the European summit meeting.

2002 Greece adopts the euro.

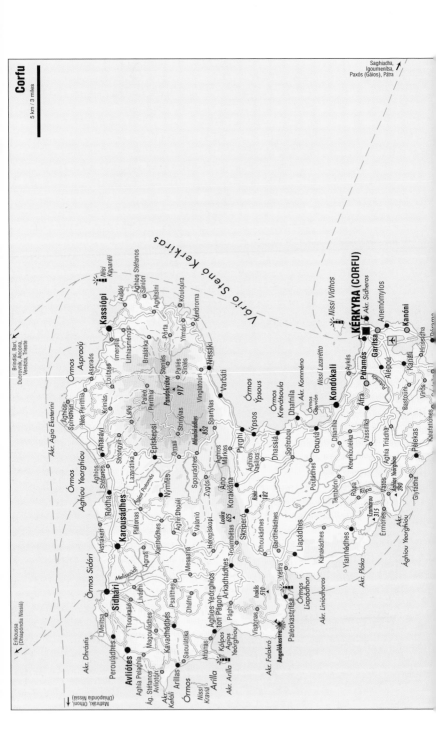

Corfu

5 km / 3 miles

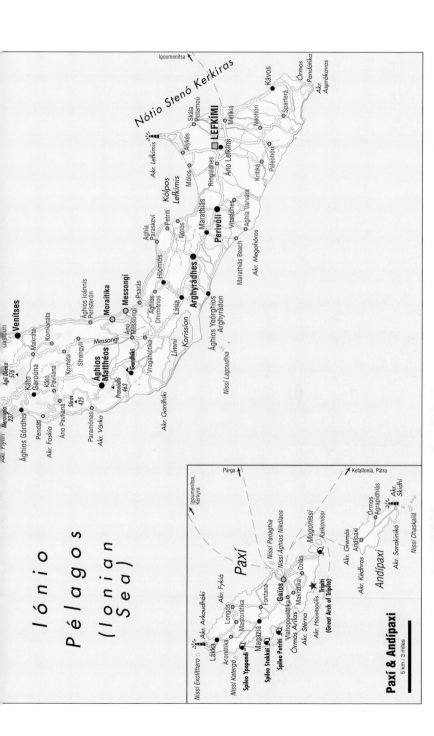

Iónio
Pélagos
(Ionian
Sea)

Nótio Stenó Kerkíras

Igoumenítsa

Venítses

Makráta
Komianáta
Gastoúri
Ákr. Fryini
Merovigli
237
Agii Deka
576
Ághios Górdhis
Pendáti
Káto
Garoúna
Áno Pavliana
Kórnáta
Strongylí
Komnáta
 Káto
Pávliana
Áno Pavliana
Paramónas
Ákr. Foskía
Ákr. Várka
Sfros
425
Prasoúdi
163
Ághios
Matthéos
Gardhíki
Ákr. Gardhíki

Ághios Ioánnis
Peristerón
Moraitika
Ano
Messongí
Messongí
Áno
Messongi
Psarás
Ághios
Dhimítrios
Vragdhiótika
Messongí
Limni
Korission
Nissí Lagoudhía

Ághios Yeórghios
Arghyrádon

Áchlos
Litiá
Áchlos

Petriti
Nótos
Aghía
Paraskeví

Argyrádhes

Perivóli

Marathiás
Vitaládhes
Aghía Varváta

Marathiás Beach
Ákr. Megahóros

Kólpos
Lefkímis

Skála
Potamoú

Akr. Lefkímis

Alykés
Ano Lefkími
Ringládhes

LEFKÍMI

Molos
Kritiká
Paleohóri

Neohóri
Melíkia
Sparterá

Kávos

Ormos
Pandánika
Ákr.
Asprókavos

Igoumenítsa

Paxí & Andípaxi

5 km / 3 miles

Párga
Kefalloniá, Pátra

Igoumenítsa,
Kérkyra

Nissí Exolítharo
Ákr. Arkoúdhaki
Lákka

Aronátika
Ákr. Fykiá
Longós
Mastorátika

Nissí Panaghía
Nissí Ághios Nikólaos

Fontana
Gaïos
Makrátika

Spileo Ypapandí
Nissí Katergó
Magaziá

Spileo Stokkíá

Spileo Peritri
Vlahopoúlatika
Ormos Arílas
Ákr. Sterna

Ákr. Housmoúlis
Tripití
(Great Arch of Tripító)

Mogoníssi
Kaïkoníssi

Ozías

Paxí

Ákr. Gremós
Andípaxi

Ormos
Agrapidhiás

Akr.
Skídhi

Ákr. Kédhros

Andípaxi

Ákr. Sarokinikó

Nissí Dhaskaliá

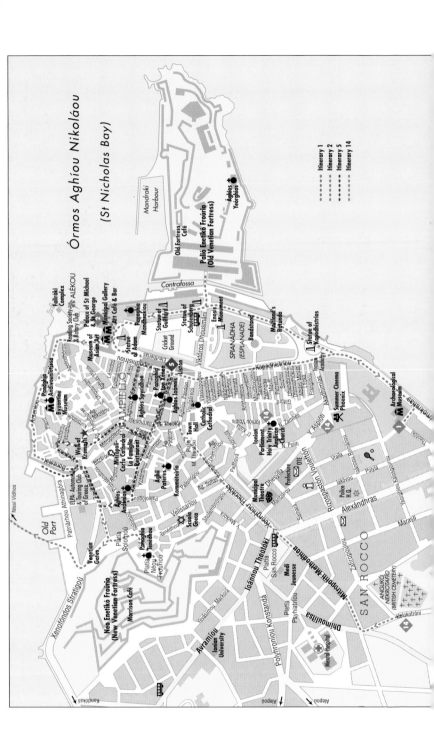

Órmos Aghíou Nikoláou

(St Nicholas Bay)

Mandraki Harbour

Contrafossa

Old Fortress Café

Paliò Enetikó Froúrio (Old Venetian Fortress)

Aghios Yeórghios

Itinerary 1
Itinerary 2
Itinerary 5
Itinerary 14

Faliráki Complex

ALÉKOU

Reading Society & Rotary Club

Palace of St Michael & St George

Museum of Asian Art

Statue of Adam

Municipal Gallery Art Café & Bar

Panaghía Mandhrákiou

Statue of Guilford

Enosi Monument

Statue of Schulenberg

Maitland's Rotonda

SPANÁDHA (ESPLANADE)

Bandstand

Statue of Kapodhistrias

Cricket Ground

Eleftherías

Víktoros Dhousmáni

Kapodhistríou

Ionian Academy

Panaghía Andivouniótissa

Byzantine Museum

CAMPIELLO

Aghios Spyridhon

Panaghía ton Xénon

Aghios Ioánnis

Catholic Cathedral

Town Hall

Ionian Parliament

Anglican Holy Trinity Church

Summer Cinema Phoenix

Archaeológikó Mouseío

Well of Kremasti

Corfu Cathedral

La Famiglia Restaurant

Aghii Patéres

Aghios Andréas

Kommotário

Venetian Gates

Platía Solohoú

Panaghía Tenédhou

Municipal Theatre

Dhesylla

Prefecture

Police H.Q.

Alexándhras

OTE

Scuola Greca

Velissaríou

Ionian University

Avramíou

Néo Enetikó Froúrio (New Venetian Fortress)

Morrison Café

Platía Néou Froúríou

Platía San Rocco

Medi Jeunesse

Platía Psychiátrou

Mental Hospital

SAN ROCCO

ANGLIKÓ NEKROTAFÍO (BRITISH CEMETERY)

Drimoússa

Mitrópolin Methodhíon

Polyhroníou Konstandá

Ináhnou Theotóki

Old Port

Patriárhou Athinagóra

ELPA - Automobile & Touring Club of Greece

Nissí Vídhos

Xenofóndos Stratigoú

Alepoú

Alepoú

Kondókali

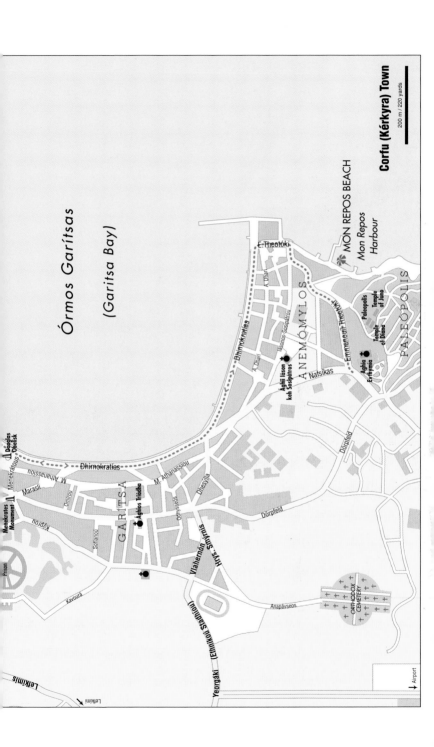

Corfu (Kérkyra) Town

200 m / 220 yards

Corfu Itineraries

1. THE HISTORIC CENTRE   *(see map, p20–1)*

This walking tour takes in the Archaeological Museum of Corfu Town (Kérkyra), the Old Fortress, the Museum of Asian Art (housed in the Palace of St Michael and St George) and the Church of the Miracle-Working St Spýridhon. Lunch on Kapodhistríou Street, an afternoon swim at Mon Repos and dinner at La Famiglia round out this full day of activities. Be sure to call and reserve a table at La Famiglia (tel: 26610 30270).

To the starting point: the corniche of Garítsa Bay, Dhimokratías Avenue, is easily accessible from all Kérkyra hotels. Follow it until, midway around the bay, between the Old Fortress to the north and the Mon Repos beach 'club' to the south, you reach Vraïla Street.

For this day's walking tour of the historic centre it is wise to first breakfast well at your hotel, or at Starenío *(see page 70)*, then set out in comfortable shoes – any day but Monday – armed with sunhat and sunblock if you are there in summer, to arrive at the Archaeological Museum of Corfu as early as possible.

The **Archaeological Museum of Corfu** (tel: 26610 30680; daily 8.30am–3pm, closed Mon; entrance fee) is situated half a block up Vraïla Street from its junction with Dhimokratías Avenue. On the ground floor are some nicely detailed small bronze statuettes dating from the Archaic, Roman and Hellenistic periods. Here too is the stunning silver ceremonial helmet of a pint-sized Hellenistic general (complete with gold myrtle-berry and acorn chaplet), together with his iron armour, swords, battle helmet, oil-scrapers (for personal hygiene), protective shoulder epaulets and bronze burial urn, all dating from the 4th century BC.

Early Cycladic (3rd millennium BC) violin-shaped marble statuettes and a marble, crater-shaped *kandhíla* (oil lamp) – recovered from thieves of Greek antiquities – complete the ground-floor displays. Plexiglas maps on the first-floor landing detail Corfu's ancient cities and archaeological sites, human habitations dating from 40,000BC up to and including the Roman period. You might want to pick up a copy of the concise history and guide, *Ancient Kérkyra*, by Alkestis Spetsieri-Choremi (available in English and German at the ticket desk), which details the island's early history and significant finds.

Proceed into the central upstairs hall, to be confronted by the prone Archaic carved Lion of the Menekrates, from the 7th century BC. The galleries to the east, accessed by a separate door from the stairway, contain a dozen or so clay figurines of the

Left: the Church of St George
Right: Corinthian lion

goddess Artemis in her avatar as the Mistress of Animals, cradling beasts ranging from deer to lion cubs. These are representative of the 6,000-plus idols found in the 480BC Temple of Artemis on the Mon Repos estate near Kanóni. In the same room is a fragment of an Archaic pediment from the 5th century BC, which depicts a Dionysian symposium – the god Dionysos, wielding a drinking horn, and a youth recline on a couch, beneath which a lion is being cornered by a hunting hound. A small limestone head of a *kouros*, dating from 535–530BC, and an early example of statuary bearing the enigmatic 'Archaic Smile', was executed by a Corinthian sculptor.

In the aqua-walled **Gorgon Room** looms the monumental Gorgon (or Medusa) Pediment, dated 590–580BC, a fragment of the Doric Temple of Artemis. A strangely Asiatic figure, Medusa, the mother of Chrysaor (the diminutive figure to the right) and the winged horse, Pegasus (formerly on her left, now missing), is frightful even by 21st-century standards, with her protuberant eyes and serpentine locks. (In myth, the hero Perseus cut off her head without looking at her directly, lest he be turned to stone, and her two offspring were born, simultaneously, of her spilt blood.)

Leave the museum now and go back to Dhimokratías Avenue, turning

left towards the Old Fortress, your next destination. Follow the corniche along the bay, passing the luxurious Corfu Palace Hotel on your left. The Old Fortress will be clearly visible for the duration of your 5- to 10-minute walk, with a backdrop of the denuded mountains of Albania.

Proceed gently uphill on the seaward side of Dhimokratías Avenue. You will be overtaken by brightly painted horse-drawn carriages, available for hire on

Above: the Gorgon Pediment
Left: Maitland Rotunda

the grand central esplanade, or 'Spianádha' ahead. Pass, on your left, a marble statue of the illustrious Corfiot, Count John Kapodhistrias, first president of the independent Greek state. Bear right along Dhimokratías Avenue, with the Spianádha on your left and the Café Aktaion on your right.

The Venetian Legacy

The **Spianádha**, Kérkyra's grand central park, serves as a meeting place for the entire capital in summer. Established by the Venetians for strategic purposes, and maintained by subsequent occupying forces, the Spianádha is now used for rest and recreation and, at the far northern end, for cricket matches in the spring and summer. Look to your left as you walk, and you will see within the park reminders of the British occupation: the Rotunda (known to the locals as the 'Stérna', as it was once the site of the town's cistern), erected in memory of the first British High Commissioner, Sir Thomas Maitland; and the Bandstand (or 'Pálko'), where open-air concerts are staged by the many Corfiot philharmonic societies – massive brass bands – throughout the summer.

Directly opposite the hire centre for horse-drawn carriages is the entrance to the **Paleó Froúrio** (Old Fortress; tel: 26610 48311; daily 9am–7pm; entrance fee). Proceed directly across the iron bridge which spans the Venetian-dug moat (the *Contrafossa*), today lined with Corfiot boat sheds and dotted with local fishing boats. To left and right, you can see massive twin bastions that were constructed by the Venetians during the 16th century. Over the Main Gate, a 19th-century inscription commissioned by King George I of the Greeks reads, 'My strength is the love of the people'.

On your left, before entering the enceinte proper, you will find an excellent **Ministry of Culture Museum Shop** (tel: 26610 46919; Mon–Fri 8.30am–3pm), a good source of information and fine souvenirs. There are casts of sculptures from many Greek museums, copies of icons from Corfu's Byzantine Museum, books, cards and reproduction jewellery. Mr Spyros Margaritis, who works here, is very knowledgeable, not only about the fortress, but also about Corfu's history in general.

On your right, do not miss the permanent exhibition entitled **Byzantine Collection of Corfu** (Mon–Fri 8.30am–3pm), also housed in the gatehouse and comprising early Christian finds from Paleopolis (near present-day Kanóni) and Káto Korakiána (in central Corfu, near Dhassiá). There are floor mosaics on display, as well as marble architectural fragments from the early basilica, and beautiful ecclesiastical wall paintings.

Entering the fortress proper you will see, to left and right, the land moat,

Right: fortified tunnel through the Old Fortress

and pass the Roman Catholic Chapel of the Madonna Dei Carmini (now used as a workshop for icon restoration). Pass beneath Corfu's Archives and Public Library, formerly the British Barracks. Proceed right, following signs for St George's Church and the **Old Fortress Café** (tel: 26610 48550; daily 9am–2am). A flight of stairs on your left takes you up by stages to the Land Tower. The café, with its splendid view of Garítsa Bay, is to your right as you ascend. It is a nice, cool place to return to for a meal or a drink – and becomes a popular late-night venue after dark.

With the Clock Tower on your left, proceed steeply uphill, passing through a fortified archway and cobbled tunnel, to view the coastline of Albania and Greek Epirus, and tiny Vídhos islet, site of the Serbian Cemetery, where some 40,000–50,000 casualties from World War I lie buried. Lazarétto islet, site of German executions of members of the Corfiot Resistance, is slightly further west.

Climb further on your right, passing the Venetian Prison. The ascent to the lighthouse is steep, but the view from the summit is worth the effort. Carefully retrace your steps to the Old Fortress Café, then proceed gently downhill to your right where you can see the imposing, spare, Parthenon-like facade of the **Church of St George of the Old Fortress** (Ághios Yeórghios tou Paleoú Frouríou). Incongruous here among the ramparts, this originally Anglican church was built during the years of the British Protectorate (1815–64), to a Doric/Georgian design (the interior was sadly altered by the Nazi bombardment of Corfu in September 1943). Converted to a Greek Orthodox sanctuary in 1865, the beautiful, simple interior affords a peaceful respite after your hike round the battlements.

itineraries

Gardens and Galleries

Now head across the vast, gravelled parade grounds, with the café uphill to your right. To the right, you'll find the way out of the Old Fortress, passing a fussy, Carraran marble statue of Field-Marshal Count Johann Matthias von der Schulenburg, the Saxon soldier of fortune who saved the day – and Corfu – when the Ottoman Turks attacked in 1716. Proceed, anti-clockwise, around the Spianádha for about 23m (75ft), where you will pass a small park with a statue of the eccentric expatriate, the 5th Earl of Guilford (1769–1828), who gave Greece its first modern university. Just beyond Guilford Park is the small terracotta-and-burgundy **Church of Panaghía Mandhrakíou.** An iron gate adjacent to the church leads into yet another garden and the Municipal Gallery's Art Café and Bar (tel: 26610 49366; daily 9.30am–midnight), which offers light snacks and beverages.

Leave the garden – you'll return to the gallery later on in your stay – and continue your ambulatory circuit of the Spianádha, now rounding the municipal cricket pitch on your left. The Municipal Art Gallery and the Museum of Asian Art are both housed in the imposing neoclassical Palace of St Michael and St George, built between 1819 and 1824 by Maltese stonemasons in honour of British citizens who served with distinction on Malta and throughout the Ionian islands. Before it, in a small park, stands a statue of British Lord High Commissioner, Sir Frederick Adam, who built an aqueduct for Kérkyra in 1832. (On summer evenings the pond at Adam's feet fills with large, noisy frogs, who sound like Aristophanes' ancient croakers.)

The **Museum of Asian Art** (tel: 26610 30443; daily 8.30am–3pm, closed Mon; entrance fee), which has been open to the public since 1923, is a distinct surprise, containing as it does fine holdings of Chinese, Japanese and Central, South and Southeast Asian art. Donated by four 20th-century Greek diplomat-collectors over a period of about 40 years, the collection is well documented in *Kerkyra: Museum of Asian Art,* by archaeologist Aglaia Karamanou-Papoutsani, which is readily available in Kérkyra.

On leaving the palace turn right, then sharp left down towards the Spianádha, watching out for oncoming traffic. The lovely colonnaded **Listón** (signed Leofóros Vasiléos Yeorghíou A) lies directly ahead – a marble-tiled pedestrian mall lined with upmarket cafés. Conceived by a Frenchman, Matthieu de Lesseps, the colonnade was built in 1807 and resembles the rue de Rivoli, with its oversized iron lanterns and covered arcade, or 'Volta'.

One street behind and parallel to the Listón is Kapodhistríou Street, and at Nos 23 and 66 respectively are two fine restaurants, the Aegli *(see page 73)* and the Rex *(see page 75),* either of which is a fine place to stop for lunch (or return for dinner). Have a discreet peek in the kitchen before you order – you're sure to see something authentically Corfiot and delicious.

Above Left: Church of Panaghía Mandhrakíou. **Left:** icons of St Spýridhon. **Right:** statue of Sir Frederick Adam

St Spýridhon's Shrine

After lunch, retrace your route along Kapodhistríou Street and turn down intersecting Agíou Spyrídonos Street. Halfway down the block, you will see, rising on your left, the crimson-topped campanile of the 1590 founded **Church**

of the Miracleworking St Spýridhon, patron saint of Corfu *(see page 16).* Quickly passing the souvenir shops, then the 18th-century Church of St Eleftherios and St Anna on your left, walk another 15m (50ft) or so till you see the unassuming entrance to St Spýridhon's. The entrance may be humble, but this structure is home to Corfu's holy of holies. Proceed, with due reverence, into the tiny room to the right of the iconostasis. Here you will be able to see the Viennese silver reliquary containing the mummified remains of the saint – which attracts Orthodox pilgrims from all over the world. As local tradition has it, the saint's slippers must be replaced periodically, when they are worn out from his supernatural visits among his flock.

Retracing your steps to the Spianádha, you have a 20- to 30-minute walk south to Mon Repos beach. Head south from the Spianádha on Dhimokratías Avenue, passing the Corfu Palace Hotel and Vraïla Street, making a complete circuit of Garítsa Bay, either along the seafront or in the shade of the avenue-long park. As you near the end of the bay, you pass the **Nautilus Café** (tel: 26610 49707; daily 8am–1am), where you can pause for a *frappé* (iced coffee) or a *tsitsibýra* (ginger beer), a non-alcoholic, refreshingly unsweet drink which, like cricket, is one of the few enduring British legacies to Corfiot life. Just one brewery in Kalafatiónes still makes it.

Afternoon at the Beach

Bear right along Emmanouíl Theotóki Street now, staying close to the water, and you come at once to the little waterfront eating and swimming club called **Mon Repos** (daily 8am–10pm; entrance fee), which has changing rooms, showers, toilets, beach umbrellas and sunbeds. The little beach can be busy in high season, but is less crowded in late afternoon. (The environs of Mon Repos comprise the site of ancient Corcyra, the ruins of an early Christian church and the 1824 villa, now a lovely house-museum, where Britain's Prince Philip was born in 1921.)

After your swim, either stop off at the Nautilus, or save yourself for La Famiglia. A relative newcomer among Kérkyra's fine Italian restaurants, **La Famiglia** (30 Maniarízi keh Arlióti Street, in the Kandoúni Bízi district; tel: 26610 30270) features spectacular pasta dishes such as seafood linguine, with fresh mature mussels and *vongole* (baby mussels); rigatoni with chicken sautéed in sweet wine and herbs; an antipasto salad with bruschetta; fresh vegetable quiches; and a devilish array of house desserts.

Above: Church of the Miracleworking St Spýridhon

itineraries

From Kapodhistríou Street, turn into Nikifórou Theotóki Street and proceed west for about three blocks, turning right into Maniarízi keh Arlióti Street: La Famiglia is just the toss of a bread roll uphill. If it is fully booked, an excellent alternative is the traditional taverna **O Yiannis** (43 Agíon Iásonos and Sosipátrou Street; tel: 26610 31066; daily 7pm–midnight, closed Sun) in the Anemomílos Quarter. Open since the late 1970s at this location, a block east of Corfu's only extant Byzantine church, dedicated to SS Jason and Sosipater, O Yiannis has preserved the time-honoured traditions of Greek tavernas of the early 20th century. You troop off to the kitchen to be shown the contents of up to two dozen 23-litre (5-gallon) cooking pots, each containing an aromatic Greek or Corfiot speciality. You make your choices – a daunting task – and sit down to such delights as veal in lemon sauce, stuffed cabbage leaves, *tsigarellí* (piquant Corfiot greens), anchovies, *bourdéto* (spicy fish soup), *sofríto* (veal in vinegar sauce), etc. This attractive, humble garden restaurant is known to everyone on the island.

At the day's end, you may want to buy a soft ice-cream cone from **Choices by Sussana** (48 Kapodhistríou Street) and find a seat on the Spianádha near the bandstand. The whole of Kérkyra gathers here of a summer's night until very, very late, and it's a supremely romantic place to sit.

2. PALACE AND NEW FORTRESS *(see map, p20–1)*

This itinerary begins with breakfast at the Art Café and Bar, then takes you to the island capital's Municipal Gallery, the Byzantine Museum and Church of Panaghía Andivouniótissa, the New Fortress and, finally, Vídhos islet, for lunch and an afternoon swim.

Start at the Art Café and Bar, in the gardens adjacent to the Municipal Gallery, at around 9.30am on any weekday but Monday. Go protected against the sun, and carry bathing gear, unless you plan to stop at your lodgings prior to the trip out to Vídhos islet.

Have breakfast in the **Art Café and Bar** gardens (tel: 26610 49366), situated to the right of the Palace of St Michael and St George, as you face it, overlooking St Nicholas Bay. Afterwards, walk round to the front of the palace and enter Kérkyra's **Municipal Art Gallery** (Dhimotikí Pinakothíki; tel: 26610 48690; daily 9am–9pm; entrance fee). In the gallery book shop you could pick up a copy of local author John Forte's *The Palace of St Michael and St George*, an entertaining history of this remarkable building.

First, enter the series of small rooms that contain travelling exhibitions of small-scale art works – often etchings, lithographs and photographs. Then, retaining your entrance ticket, retrace your steps to the Art Café and Bar gardens and enter the picture gallery up a double flight of stone steps. Just below the café here, down a sinuous iron staircase, is a nice little swimming area known as Faliráki or **Ta Bánia tou Alékou**

Right: lunch is in the bag

and a café called **En Plo** (tel: 26610 81813; daily around 10am–2am, year round), which is a pleasant place for a snack and swim later in your visit, if you are staying in Kérkyra.

The Municipal Art Gallery holdings consist of significant works by noteworthy Cretan and Corfiot School painters. Particularly notable are the late 16th- to early 17th-century icons on wood, *Noli me Tangere,* by Cretan School iconographer Emmanuel Lambardos, and Michael Damaskinos's *The Stoning of St Stephen* (1591) and *The Decapitation of John the Baptist* (1592). You'll find them by turning right at the museum entrance. After viewing these, you should seek out the superb 19th-century oils by Paul Prossalendis The Younger (1857–94), specifically his two portraits of Arab musicians (1880 and 1882), and a Corfiot seascape (1881). The formal palace rooms that are home to this gallery are also worth studying. Corfiot watercolours – a longstanding artistic tradition on the island – are well represented in works by Angelos Giallinas (1857–1939), who established The Corfiot School of Fine Arts in 1902. For both wings of the museum a bilingual Greek-English catalogue is available.

Leave the gallery and gardens of the Art Café and Bar and walk along the entire front colonnade of the palace, passing through the western gate (also a thoroughfare for motorised traffic) and head northwest along Dhimokratías Avenue as far as the Old Port. Keep close to the bay, looking out towards lovely Vídhos islet, where you will be going later. Dhimokratías Avenue metamorphoses a number of times along your route, initially into Arseníou Street.

Ecclesiastical Treasures

About 400m (¼ mile) northwest of the palace, left up several flights of broad stone steps, is the **Byzantine Museum** and **Church of Panaghía Andivouni-ótissa** (tel: 26610 38313; daily 9am–3pm, closed Mon; entrance fee). This ecclesiastical structure, whose name means 'The Virgin Opposite the Mountain', was built in the 15th century, and now houses remarkable icons by Cretan School iconographers such as Emmanuel Zanes, Stephanos Tzangarolas and Emmanuel Lombardos. The aisleless, timber-roofed basilica is characteristic of the Ionian Island type, with painted 'wallpaper', and a ceiling rich in gilded carvings. The resting place of generations of Corfiot nobles, the church was, in essence, donated to the Greek state as a museum by some of the island's first families, and is a treasure trove of Greek Orthodox art.

After leaving the museum, continue your westward circuit of the port on Arseníou Street. As Arseníou becomes Donzelót Street, you will see the New Fortress looming ahead of you, another 400m (¼ mile) down the corniche. On the left, you will pass one of the four entrances to the old Venetian city, the so-called **Spiliá Gate** (Cave Gate), a fortified tunnel through the city walls. On your right is a little park and beyond that, the quays. Turn sharply left at the foot of Donzelót Street into the little Square of the New Fortress (Platía Néou Frouríou). You'll see, to your right, jacaranda trees, which flower profusely in spring and early summer, and a checkpoint for the Greek Naval Station. Pass on through the square, heading south about 15m (50ft), then turn right up Solomoú Street. Slightly up the hill from here, you pass the baroque, salmon-pink and terracotta Roman Catholic **Church of Panaghía Tenédhou**, with its inscribed marble portal.

Bastion of the Serenissima

Just up the steps beside the church is the entrance to the **New Fortress** (tel: 26610 27370; daily 9am–7pm; entrance fee). Your ascent, through fortified tunnels – note the ingenious drainage system – and across the dry moat, is gentle, but the midday sun is formidable, so seek shade if you can. The fortress, also known as the Fortress of St Mark – with the lions of The Most Serene Republic floating above its gates – was begun by the Venetians in 1576, only 26 years later than the Old Fortress, after the second siege of the island by the Ottoman Turks. The Venetians completed their work in 1588; the British added the high citadel in 1815.

The Venetians transformed Kérkyra into an incomparable system of defences and a watching station par excellence: the views in all directions from the New Fortress are panoramic. The galleries occasionally host events and exhibits, and the Morrison Café here is a current favourite of young Corfiots after dark. Having toured both fortresses, you will have a better appre-

Top Left: up to the picture gallery
Left: the Bánia tou Alékou. **Right:** caïque to Vídhos

ciation of the scope of the Venetian ramparts. The forts were linked by a huge circuit of fortified double walls which entirely encircled the town. Underground passageways – perhaps stretching as far as Vídhos islet – enabled all those in the extended garrison to communicate back and forth in time of siege.

From the Old Port quays near Spiliá Park, caïques leave for Vídhos islet every half hour or so. Ask to be directed to *'tó kaïki yia Víthos'* (tel: 26610 44222 for information, but only in Greek). After an easy 15-minute crossing, you reach **Vídhos**, once hotly contested and fortified (by Turkish, Vene-

tian, French, Russian and British invaders, among others), but now primarily a summer picnic destination for Corfiots – and final resting place for thousands of Serb soldiers who died at Corfu after an arduous retreat across Albania in 1916. A humble taverna here, open in summer, is a good place for lunch. Have a meal and a swim and enjoy the pretty views of Kérkyra from the sea.

3. THE AHILLION AND DHASSIA *(see map, p33)*

This itinerary comprises a tour of the Empress Elisabeth's residence on Corfu, the Ahíllion, and a visit to the seaside resort of Dhassiá for an afternoon swim.

To starting point: at your Kérkyra hotel, have the desk call a radio taxi to take you to the Ahíllion, 10km (6 miles) south of the capital in the hillside village of Gastoúri. Take sun protection and bathing gear along.

Your taxi will take you through Kérkyra's unremarkable but bustling suburbs, passing the airport en route. Already, though, you will begin to get some idea of the lushness of this Ionian island, where even the most humble residences are surrounded by roses and bougainvillaea, and cypress-studded olive groves abound.

You will wend your way through the hamlet of Gastoúri before your driver lets you off at the main gate and ticket booth of the **Ahíllion** (tel: 26610 56210; daily 8am–7pm; entrance fee). Surrounded by a hilltop garden floating in rich olive groves, this imposing, if capricious, stately home was the dream-come-true of Empress Elisabeth of Austria (1837–98). Erected in 1890–91, and designed by Italian architects Raphael Carito and Antonio Landi, the structure is a Pompeiian pastiche of dizzying complexity and

Above a triumphant Achilles

itineraries

dubious taste, but the empress's passion for her Homeric hero, Achilles, for whom the mansion was named, is evident.

As Empress Elisabeth wrote: 'I dedicate this palace to him because for me he represents the Greek spirit, the beauty of the land and of the people of this place. I loved him because he was swift-footed like Hermes, powerful, proud and strong-willed like a Greek mountain and because, fast as the wind as he was, he defied all kings, customs and laws.'

Destined to enjoy her idyllic Corfiot retreat for only six years, the empress was assassinated by a knife-wielding Italian anarchist in Geneva on 10 September 1898, and died there at the Beau Rivage Hotel.

In 1908, her stately folly was purchased by another royal philhellene, Elisabeth's cousin, Kaiser Wilhelm II, who added his own version of Achilles to the garden, extensively renovated the mansion and improved its grounds. The kaiser spent a total of 162 days at the Ahíllion during his own six years of ownership, sailing away from Corfu for good in 1914. Three months after his departure, he declared war on France. The following day, Great Britain declared war on Germany. Four years later, Kaiser Wilhelm abdicated, fled to exile in The Netherlands – and never returned to Corfu.

Memories of Empress and Kaiser

Students of early 20th-century history will find the ground floor of the Ahíllion, which today houses some of the personal effects of both the Empress Elisabeth and the kaiser, fascinating. The furnishings are monumentally gauche, but the kaiser's writing desk and washstand, paintings of Wilhelm at the Ahíllion and of the imperial yacht, the *Hohenzollern*, intimate portraits of Elisabeth, with her flowing, knee-length locks, and displays of some of the empress's jewellery, are all strangely compelling.

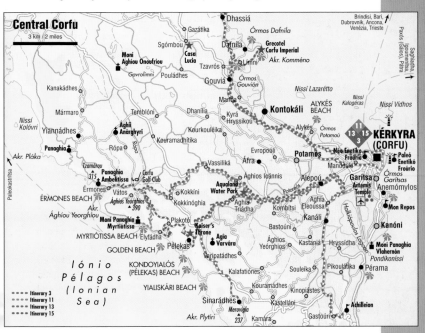

In the gardens, be sure to see the touching marble, *The Dying Achilles*, that Elisabeth commissioned from the German sculptor Ernst Herther in 1884, and the monumental *Achilles Triumphant*, with its gold-plated spear and helmet, an over-the-top bronze by German sculptor Johannes Gotz. The kaiser's inscription, removed by the French during World War II, read: 'This man, Achilles, son of Peleus, was erected by Germany's Wilhelm, for future generations to remember.'

The gardens, now largely closed to the public, are redolent of forsythia, jasmine and magnolia. From the portico, lined with marbles depicting the Nine Muses, the Three Graces, and renowned poets and playwrights, peek back into the Ahíllion at an immense oil (4m by 11m/13ft by 36ft) by Austrian painter Franz von Match depicting Achilles dragging the body of Troy's Prince Hector around the city's walls. One of the grand moments of Homer's *Iliad*, the scene shows the Argives' champion, Achilles, at his best – and worst.

By Bus to the Beach

A kiosk located at the downhill end of a row of tatty tourist shops sells tickets for the Gastoúri-Kérkyra bus. Ask for directions to the bus stop and departure times for the No 10 blue bus (tickets are very reasonably priced for all island bus routes). Alternatively, taxis regularly deposit visitors at the Ahíllion, and are only too happy to find a return fare to town. Ask for Platía Saróko (San Rocco Square). The bus or taxi will leave you in town at the main blue bus terminus on Yeorgíou Theotóki, or San Rocco Square.

If you do not have your bathing gear, or are hungry, you may choose to return to your lodgings now, and/or break for lunch. The Rex or the Aegli restaurants, both located on Kapodhistríou Street behind the Listón, are both excellent choices at midday.

Return to San Rocco Square and ask for directions to the No 7 bus stop (tickets are available at a kiosk on the square). The No 7 blue bus for Dhassiá leaves about every 20 minutes from San Rócco, passing small seaside tourist hotels, olive groves and grand resorts on its 25-minute journey north. The area immediately north of Kérkyra is heavily developed, as is the sea-

side resort village of **Dhassiá** itself (this is the location of the former Club Mediterranée). The bus stops just outside the Elea Beach Hotel. Facing the hotel, proceed left down a paved road for about 45m (150ft), then turn sharply right down a gravel path to the beach. About 1.5km (1 mile) of pebbled beach, dotted with cafés and bars, watersport piers and umbrella and sunbed vendors awaits you. It's often more peaceful towards the far left, the Club Med end of the beach.

When you've had enough of sun and sea, retrace your steps to the Dhassiá bus stop and head back into town.

4. KANONI AND MOUNT PANDOKRATOR *(see map, p36)*

The day begins with a little jaunt by taxi, on foot and by ferry boat or caïque to the little 'suburb' of Kanóni, the church and monastery of Panaghía Vlahernón and Pondikoníssi, or 'Mouse Island'. Later, we take an afternoon-into-sunset journey by hire car to the mountain and monastery named for the Pandokrátor, or the Ruler of All.

To starting point: parking is a problem near to the starting point, so arrange to pick up a hire car later in the afternoon, and then take a taxi from Kérkyra to Kanóni. Ask to be let out at the Kafeneion *(café) Kanoni. Wear comfortable shoes and modest dress, and take along beach gear and sun protection if you leave early enough to fit in a swim off Pondikoníssi.*

Kanóni gets its name from an iron cannon *(kanóni)* left behind here by the French army (not the cannon that now sits in front of the café, which is Russian and only a few decades old). The hamlet is on a promontory overlooking the Halkiópoulos Lagoon and the two islets of Vlahérna and Pondikoníssi, the former islet being the hallmark Corfiot image burned on the memory of every visitor to this island since the 1960s. Behind the open-air café – which you'll need to walk through – a flight of marble steps leads down to the jetty connecting Vlahérna islet to Corfu proper. Your descent takes all of three minutes, but it's slippery.

Miracle of the Virgin

Built in 1685, the tiny church and monastery of **Panagía Vlahernón**, with its pretty Venetian belfry, is named for its miracle-working icon of the Virgin. Legend has it that Mary appeared in a dream to a Corfiot man, telling

Left: lightly tanned at Dhassiá. **Above:** the church and monastery of Panaghía Vlahernón. **Right:** boat to Pondikoníssi

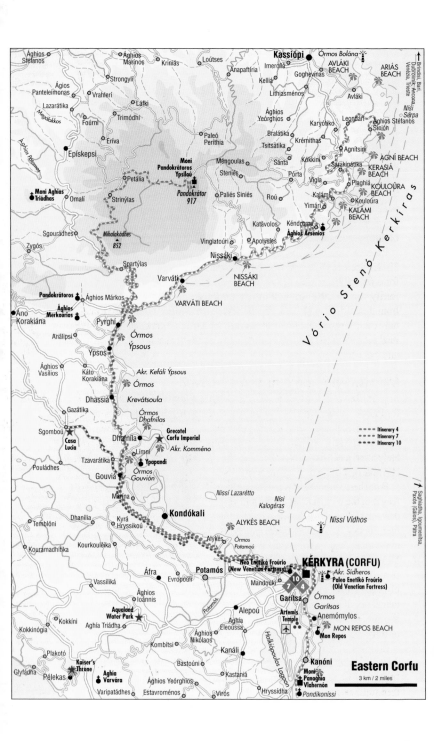

Eastern Corfu

3 km / 2 miles

itineraries

him that her icon had been stolen from a famous church dedicated to her in Constantinople, then left in or lost off the coast of Corfu. The man awoke, retrieved the icon, and a church was duly erected, with the same name as the icon's 5th-century Byzantine mother-church in what is today Istanbul. The Virgin's icon is festooned with *támmata* – gold, silver and tin votive offerings, left by the faithful in gratitude for answered prayers. Go in, see the icon, make a small donation, and light a beeswax candle, leaving it in the candle stand. Only one monk makes his home here now, and he's not much in evidence.

Back on the narrow concrete causeway, you will see little ferries and caïques leaving, every half hour or so in high season, for tiny **Pondikoníssi**, with its 11th- to 12th-century Byzantine **Church of the Pandokrátor**. It's a pleasant, 10-minute crossing out to the islet in the bay, where you can peek inside the church, or have a dip in the sea if you wish. Lamentably, Corfu's airport, adjacent to Kanóni, has permanently shattered the peace of this once-silent corner of the island.

Proceed back up the marble steps to the **Kafeneion Kanoni** (tel: 26610 39743; open all day), in business here since 1864, and a good place to stop for a *frappé* (iced coffee) and a slice of *sokolattína* (chocolate torte) to fortify you for the journey to Mount Pandokrátor. Incidentally, just uphill from the café is the Corfu Holiday Palace Hotel, which houses the island's only casino, should you wish to return here much, much later for less spiritual pursuits. You will need to hail a taxi and return to town to pick up your hire car a couple of hours before sunset.

Monastery on the Roof of the Island

In your hire car, leave Kérkyra via the New Port, initially following signings for Paleokastrítsa, which will take you north. After about 10km (6 miles), turn right for Dhassiá and Kassiópi. After another 2km (1¼ mile), you will pass the seaside resort town of Dhassiá and the Club Mediterranée, then immediately afterwards the busy resort of Ýpsos, directly on the sea. After 2.5km (1½ miles), turn sharply left for Spartýlas.

From here spectacular views open along the length of the east coast of Corfu, and you will drive past many private villas (including the inexplicably named Villa Hermaphrodite), but make sure you save some film for the summit. You will need to watch out for opposing traffic on this narrow, winding road (it's probably a good idea to hoot your horn approaching the blind, narrow curves). Drystone walls abound here, and olive trees seem to grow out of solid rock, standing on tiptoes of root.

In about 4km (2½ miles), after passing a roadside shrine on your right, you will enter the 'vertical village' of Spartýlas. Look for, and then follow signs, initially for the Monastery of Pandokrátoros Ypsiloú, and then for the

Right: a monk's perspective

villages of Petalía (7km/4¼ miles) and Láfki (12km/7½ miles). The views broaden as you approach the treeline, and a transmitting station looms on your left to remind you that you are in the 21st century. For a stretch here, some 30km (18 miles) from Kérkyra, views of the coastline open, and the landscape below is washed with every green in a summer painter's palette.

On top of the island, about 500m (¼ mile) further on, you enter a lovely high meadow ringed by peaks, with a 19th-century church off to your right. Stop to enjoy (but not to pick!) the wildflowers here, in season. Pass through the village of Strinýlas (make a note of the Elm Tree Taverna for dinner later), heading slightly downhill, following signs on the right for the monastery. Ahead of you now you will see the island's military listening station and its mast (Eiffel Tower as rendered by El Greco) atop the massif. The temperature drops as you ascend, traversing the vast rock garden, studded with odoriferous goats, that is the the roof of Corfu. Approaching the rocky summit, you'll see buildings rising out of the grey stone. Albania, vast and denuded, appears on your left.

At 917m (3,008ft) the **Monastery of Pandokrátoros Ypsiloú**, originally dating from the 16th century, coexists somewhat incongruously with the red-and-white radio tower, but enjoys views of all Corfu, the Dhiapóndia islets far to the west, Albania and Greek Epirus. The intimate space of the main church is filled with frescoes and 14th-century icons and has an impressive, silver-chased 18th-century iconostasis. The interior is more interesting than the bland exterior implies, so go in and have a look round. Outside the monastery gate is the Café Snack Bar Pantokrator – a bit profane, perhaps, but a welcome retreat from the sun and wind, and it does have a magnificent view.

Now retrace your route down the mountain to Strinýlas and the **Elm Tree Taverna** (tel: 26630 71454; daily 8am–midnight). Run by the Koskinas family, this excellent taverna specialises in grilled meats from the mainland city of Ioánnina – *sofríto*, and wild boar *stifádo*. Don't miss the wines, produced and bottled by the family. Next to the Elm Tree, call in at a little gift shop called The Olive Wood, also run by the Koskinas family. Here you'll find cutting boards, spoons, beads – even ersatz American-Indian dreamcatchers – all made from olive wood. Head downhill and back to Kérkyra, following all signs for the town as you go.

5. THE CAMPIELLO QUARTER *(see map, p20)*

This walking tour takes in the churches and squares of the quaint, colourful, centuries-old Campiello Quarter of Kérkyra.

Starting point: the corner of Nikifórou Theotóki and Kapodhistríou streets.

The historic town's main thoroughfare, connecting the Old and New Fortresses, is **Nikifórou Theotóki Street**. It also leads west to one of the four main entrances to the Venetian town, the Spilia Gate. (The other surviving portal through the great Venetian double walls is the St Nicholas Gate, located at Faliráki, or 'Bánia tou Alékou', beneath the Old Fortress on the sea.)

Proceed west on Nikifórou Theotóki Street. No 10 was the birthplace of two prominent Corfiots: Andreas Marmoras, a great local historian, in the 17th century, and George Theotokis, who was prime minister of Greece in the first decade of the 20th century. Today, the building is home to one of the island's oldest and most famous marching bands, the Philharmonic Society. On the right, in this first long block, is the **Church of ton Xenón** (Virgin of the Foreigners) and on the left, the **Church of Panagía Ágios Ioánnis** (St John the Baptist). Both churches are basilicas, with three naves. At St John's, behind glass in the wall, there is a much-kissed icon depicting the Dormition of the Virgin.

The little square in front of Panagía ton Xenón is known either as **Platía Yeorgíou Theotóki**, or the Square of the Heroes of the Cypriot Struggle. (It is also a *plakádho*, in Corfiot dialect the kind paved with marble paving stones; those paved with beach stones are called *kovoládho*.) The statue in the square, festooned with pigeons, is of George Theotokis. Proceed west, passing, at No 32, the **Papayeorghis Shop**, which sells traditional sweets and liqueurs, such as *mandóles*, *mandoláto* and kumquat liqueurs and preserves: stop and make a purchase to nibble on now or to take home as a gift. Look up now, on your right, at No 31, an old Venetian structure that has survived here for five centuries. In the small, dead-end street just beyond No 31, the British author Lawrence Durrell resided for part of his Corfiot stay (between 1935 and 1939).

Saintly Devotion and Pagan Superstition

Look up again, at the junction of four streets, for three hanging and/or painted *pínia* (pine cones). This area, called Pínia, was the centre of the old Venetian town. According to tradition, pines and pine cones are sacred to St Spýridhon *(see page 16)*, and the first families of Corfu displayed pine cones outside their homes to demonstrate their love for their island's patron saint. At the corner of Nikifórou Theotóki and Aghías Varváras streets is the Church

Left: view from Mount Pandokrátor
Right: window on the world

of SS Basil and Stephen. The building opposite the church is ornamented with *maskerónia*, or *mouryónia* – masks which, according to an ancient Roman custom, warded off evil. This building was part of the vast holdings of the Cobici family. A side entrance at No 3 Maniarízi keh Arlióti also has a pine cone. There is also a wonderful Italian restaurant in this street, at No 30: **La Famiglia**.

A tiny alley that leads down on your right now was the well-trodden route to the famous early 20th-century house of ill repute, **Lemoniá**. This block, beyond Maniarízi keh Arlióti Street, was built by the British, but in the old Venetian style. The second short street leads to the square of Lemoniá, with its lemon and mulberry trees. This area was largely razed by the Germans in World War II.

Near the west end of Nikifórou Theotóki Street, up a little flight of stairs behind an ornate wrought iron gate, is the Roman Catholic **Church of St Francis** (Ághios Frangískas). Step up into the little exterior courtyard and look at the clever drainage system here: one of the town's largest cisterns is located just below you. At the end of the street, on the right, is the town's oldest church, **Ághios Andónios** (St Anthony's), dating from the mid-16th century. An old Corfiot saying went, 'Only the old recall the sea at St Anthony's' because, in the 15th century, the sea did indeed reach this point in the town.

Turn right in front of the church into a continuation of Nikifórou Theotóki Street. On your left was the boundary of the Jewish ghetto in Venetian times (and the entrance to the New Fortress). Since the Nazi deportation of 1944 the community numbers barely 50, and the **Scuola Greca** synagogue surviving at Velissaríou is seldom used. Straight ahead now is the **Spilia Gate**, the *Pórta Spiliá*. If you're lucky, you'll hear the Third Philharmonic Society practising their brass band music near here. Within the gate proper is a little shrine to the Virgin which contains an icon that is said to work miracles.

Old Port and Sea Walls

Head northeast and you will find yourself on Donzelót Street, in the Old Port locality. Turn right, passing the Hotel Konstantinoupolis, built in 1859 and, at No 1, the modern *Efetió* or Courthouse. Continue around the port on

Above: festooned with washing.

Donzelót Street and on your right, a block south, you will arrive at Corfu's Greek Orthodox **Cathedral (Mitrópoli)**, dedicated to the Panaghía Spiliótissa (The Virgin of the Cave) and St Theodora (the Empress of Byzantium). The Cathedral houses the headless relics of St Theodora – on her name day, the Corfiots celebrate by eating watermelon, as they believe this will somehow assist their decapitated Theodora through some form of sympathetic magic.

The area north of the Cathedral, towards the sea, is known as **Mourághia** (Embankments), as the Venetian fortification indeed formed sea walls here, extending east to Faliráki. The **Café Yiali** (6 Patriárhou Athinagóra Street; tel: 26610 25650) makes a romantic spot from which to view the sunset over the **Old Port**; stop here for refreshments. Climb up some steps to Donzelót Street and turn back into the Campiello Quarter via the little alley-way called Ypapandís Street. Turn immediately left here and on your left you will see a lovely stone balcony and a tiny square – 3rd Párodhos Ypapandís Square (*párodhos* means alleyway); then comes 4th Párodhos Ypapandís Street. Here you can see the remains of more **Venetian walls**. Here, too, once stood the house of Dionysios Solomos, who wrote Greece's national anthem.

Proceed gently uphill and east, parallel to the Mourághia. Turn right into 4th Párodhos Arsoníou Street, and examine the typical, tall, Venetian-style buildings here. The true Venetian structures have very low portals and defensive window shutters. Look up at the centuries-old clothes-drying system still utilised here, whereby clothes lines are strung between the windows of facing buildings.

Take the first left and then immediately go right under a series of arches. The exterior staircases and *foursoúsia* – stone yard-arms from which planters of flowers were hung by the Venetians – are characteristic of the quarter. You will now enter a little square with a lone palm tree. Cross the square towards a raspberry-hued building behind the palm. Turn left, passing the Crêperie/Wine Bar Campiello on your right, then turn right at the corner and head down the steps to the **Square of Kremastí** (Suspended One). The church here is called the Panaghía Kremastí (Suspended Virgin). There are two explanations for this name: either it derives from an icon of the Virgin or Christ on the Cross that was displayed here, or the Venetians used this square for executions. Today, the excellent **Venetian Well** restaurant dominates the square.

Leaving Platía Kremastí, with the Venetian Well restaurant on your right, proceed downhill on 4th Párodhos Komninón Street. Turn right into Aghías Theodhóras Street, where you will see above you more *fouroúsia*, then high corbelled arches and, on your left, a solitary *maskaróni* embedded into a house reputed to have once belonged to John Kapodhistrias. Turn left into Filellínon Street, today a busy tourist shopping thoroughfare. At No 18 stands the mid-17th-century house of the Mastrakas family, with its

ΓΕΩΡΓΙΟΣ ΘΕΟΤΟΚΗΣ

Left: George Theotokis commemorated in his own square.

carved portal and beautiful balconies. The entire street is *plakádho*, paved in marble paving stones. Turn right into 3rd Párodhos Arlióti Street, and you are back at the La Famiglia restaurant. From here wend your way downhill back to Nikifórou Theotóki Street, and you're back where you began.

6. BY HYDROFOIL TO PAXÍ *(see map, p43)*

This is a day-long excursion by hydrofoil to the idyllic island of Paxí.

To the starting point: The night prior to your departure have your hotel desk arrange for a taxi to take you to the hydrofoil quay in Kérkyra's New Port. The hydrofoil for the islands of Paxí and Andípaxí leaves early, between 7 and 8.30am depending on the day of the week. Take along sun protection and beach gear – and your driving licence, in case you decide to hire a car for the day. There is also a seaplane service to Paxí, departing from Gaïos Marina (AirSea Lines, tel: 26610 49800/99316; c.€100 round trip).

Purchase a return ticket (approx. €30) on the quay, and be sure to board the right hydrofoil for Paxí (Paxós) – several hydrofoils operate from this quay and it's easy to board the wrong craft. Also be sure, once you arrive on Paxí, to enquire about the hydrofoil's precise return time in the late afternoon.

The journey from Kérkyra to the port of Gaïos on Paxí takes about an hour, unless – as sometimes happens – there's a detour to Igoumenítsa. Only sailboats and small launches dock at Gaïos proper, passing through the fjord-like entry channel. Hydrofoils dock 1km (½ mile) away, from where you can either take the scenic, shoreline walk or catch a taxi into the town.

Gaïos is a busy, charming, human-scaled port on tiny Paxí, a place that still looks like a proper Greek island town should. In fact, all of Paxí seems

dedicated to the azure sea and the olive, as opposed to the acquisition of foreign currency. Stop on the main square, near the Church of the Annunciation, for morning coffee at Center Snack Bar (tel: 26620 32698; daily) or, just off the port, at the Café Kalimera Espresso Bar (tel: 69784 19021).

Again, a stone's through from the main square is Litsa and Marina Petsali's **Tesoro** (tel: 69760 38380), a charming shop selling handmade jewellery and glassware. Nearby **Ble** (tel: 26620 32746) features Stella Christomoglou's ceramics and her son Loannis Kouvelis's small sculptures in bronze. At **Natural Traditional Products of Paxos** (tel: 26620 32320), pick up

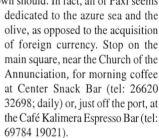

Above: swimming off Paxí

honey, olive oil, marmalade, soap and wine produced locally.

Now ask to be directed to **Paxos Magic Holidays**, where the Grammatikos family will help you with your lodging and transport needs on the island (tel: 26620 32269; fax: 26620 32122; www.paxosmagic.com). After that, set out to explore the island, from Gaïos to Fondána to Longós to Lákka. There are two attractive beaches – Kamína and Kakí Langádha – just north of Gaïos. At the beginning and end of the season, you will have them to yourself.

It's only 6.5km (4 miles) from here to the pretty port town of **Longós**, where you can walk to Levréhio beach. By far the best restaurant in Longós is **Vassilis**, at the narrowest point of the quay (tel: 26620 31587). Here, too, with its incomparable, dreamlike sea view, is the Café Bar To Taxidi (tel: 26620 31326; Easter–Oct, daily 1pm–2am).

Some 4km (2½ miles) further north is the port of **Lákka**, with a yacht marina, beaches and shops. **La Bocca** (tel: 26620 31991), to the far right end of Lákka harbour, is the creation of Torino-born, Paris-seasoned chef, Valter De Cian. The menu, wine list and view are all spectacular. Stop in, too, at **Il Pareo** (tel: 26620 30046), which stocks Far Eastern clothing, accessories, linens and an astonishing array of *pareos*.

If you want to visit Andípaxi, you can arrange transport through Paxos Magic Holidays, but you will not be able to get back to Corfu the same day. Should you decide to stay on Paxí overnight, or want to come back for a longer stay, Ms Villy Malami's **Pithari Villas** (Gaïos, Paxí, 49082, Greece; tel/fax: 26620 32491; 69448 27220; e-mail: info@pitharivillas.gr; www.pitharivillas.gr) make a wonderful place to stay, only 50m/yds from the marina (*see page 90*). The two places to dine in Gaïos are **Mambo** (tel: 26620 32670), for Greek specialities, right on the old harbour, and **Taka-Taka** (tel: 26620 32329), where you can dine on spit-roasted meats in a flower-filled garden.

Paxí and Andípaxi

5 km / 3 miles

Above: the owners of Il Pareo

7. AGHIOS STEFANOS SINION AND AGNI *(see map, p36)*

A sybaritic and gastronomic itinerary by rented car to the picturesque beach hamlets of Ághios Stéfanos Sinión and Agní, for sunbathing, boating, swimming – and especially for fine cuisine.

To the starting point: leave Kérkyra via the New Port, and head north following signs for Kassiópi all the way up Corfu's northeast coast. After about 30km (18 miles) turn right at signs for Ághios Stéfanos Sinión. To reach Agní later on, you will have to get back on the main road and proceed south for some 5km (3 miles) before turning left down a poor secondary road for Agní Beach.

One of several Corfiot towns named after St Stephen (to whom Corfu's first Christian church was dedicated), **Ághios Stéfanos Sinión** is a beautiful, peaceful little fishing village on a minute stretch of beach, just north of Jacob Rothschild's Corfiot hideaway. Stop on the pebbled beach for a swim, and have a bite to eat at the **Eucalyptus** (tel: 26630 82007; May–Oct, 8am–late), perhaps pan-fried or grilled whitebait or red mullet. There are a couple of nice bars here as well – should you decide to stay over and be looking for something to do in the evening.

Ághios Stéfanos is frequented by small yacht flotillas in season, and you can hire small motorboats on the beach and visit nearby beachlets inaccessible except by sea. (Albania is a stone's throw away from the Corfiot coast here, but *do not* attempt to land there.) If the place takes your fancy, go along to the **Kochili Restaurant** at the southern end of the beach. Helen and Yerasimos Tsirimiagos rent rooms and apartments just up the hill from the restaurant, and should be able to find you a place to stay at short notice, except at the height of the season. Alternatively, between Ághios Stéfanos Sinión and Kerasiá (the next beach down the coast) Mr Theophanis Hondroyannis has a few apartments to rent in an idyllic olive grove (Aliki Apartments; tel: 26630 81966 or 26610 4856).

Now, if you've had a swim and a light lunch at Ághios Stéfanos Sinión, and are heading back to Kérkyra around dinnertime, turn left off the main Kérkyra road after about 12km (7½ miles) and proceed for 3km (2 miles) to tiny **Agní Beach**, where you will find a couple of the best tavernas on the island.

Right on the pebble beach is **Toula** (tel: 26630 91350; 10am–5pm, 7–11pm in season), which has been owned and operated by Ms Toula Vergheti since 1982. Before that the building was an olive press belonging to Toula's father. Justly renowned in the foreign press for her prawns and mussels, Toula also concocts fabulous chocolate crêpes. Next door is the **Taverna Agni** (tel: 26630 91142), where the king prawn *saganaki*, garlic prawns, and lamb pie are all excellent.

Above: elegant Corfiot
Right: the cliffs at Sidhári

8. BY CAIQUE TO ERIKOUSSA ISLET *(see map, p46)*

This excursion, by hire car then caïque or ferry, takes in the north-western resort town of Sidhári and the Dhiapóndian islet of Eríkoussa, where you can enjoy a swim and a bracing walk round the islet.

To the starting point: well in advance of your voyage, ask your hotel concierge, or Anna Aperghi, of Aperghi Travel, to call either of the caïque skippers who make the short, daily run to Erikoussa, and ask for details of sailing times and departure points. Mr Nikos Leontitzis (tel: 6944999771) departs from the port at Sidhári Wednesday at 10am, Saturday at 10.30am and Sunday at 10am. (On the main street in Sidhári turn left to the caïque pier between the Image Photoshop and Ioanna's Corner gift shop – a tiny sign points the way to the 'Limani', or port.) Mr Dimitris Aspiotis (tel: 6932445395) departs from the shore at Ághios Stéfanos Avlioton on Monday at 8am and Friday at 10.30am. You'll need to get an early start from Corfu Town. Hire a car in Kérkyra and set out early for the 37-km (23-mile) drive to Sidhári, leaving town via the Old and the New Port. Take beach gear and sun protection, water bottles, fruit and snacks – preferably in a backpack.

Leave town to the west, then north, using Dhimokratías Avenue. Pass the Old Fortress, then drive through the portico/colonnade of the Palace of St Michael and St George. Dhimokratías soon metamorphoses into Arseníou Street, then Donzelót Street, then Zavitsianoú Street. Hug the bay, passing the New Fortress on your left. Ferries and hydrofoils leave the Old Port quays here for Italy, the Greek mainland and Paxí. Follow signs for Paleokastrítsa. You will be retracing the blue bus route to Dhassiá *(see page 32)*, until you turn off to the west at Tzavarátika. Then bear right, following signs for Sidhári, and pass through the village of Skriperó, with Mt Pandokrátor on your right. The road winds up above the olive-carpeted valley. At the village of Troumbétas (Trumpet), cross the spine of Pandokrátor, and begin your descent to the northern coast of the island.

You pass through several hillside hamlets until the road drops to the littoral and you enter the resort of **Sidhári**. Drive through the town, keep-

ing close to the shore, and turn right at The Three Little Pigs Restaurant. At Maria's Restaurant/Cocktail Bar you have access to Sidhári's once-pristine beach and the famous **Canal d'Amour** area of dramatically eroded headlands.

Sidhári has succumbed to tourist tat. It's a 'chips with everything' sort of place in high season, but you may choose to have a swim here another time.

Across the Water to Eríkoussa

Having prearranged your boat trip with one of your two skippers, you will be taking a caïque or ferry to Eríkoussa (named after the indigenous briar heath) islet, one of the three small **Dhiapóndia** islets 11 sea miles northwest of Corfu. Inhabited by some 150 Corfiot-Americans, who made their fortunes in the United States, then repatriated, Eríkoussa has its own mayor and school but, for the most part, its young people return to Astoria in New York City for the winter. There are two places to stay: the **Erikoussa Hotel** (tel: 26630 71555), and rooms at the **Anemomylos Taverna** (tel: 26630 71555/71110).

Your travel agent *(see page 96)* can arrange accommodation in private villas in or near Sidhári and Ághios Stéfanos. If you do stay in the area, note that 2km (1¼ miles) west of Sidhári is the village of Perouládhes and cliff-bottom Sunset Beach, a nice place to swim and enjoy the beautiful sun-

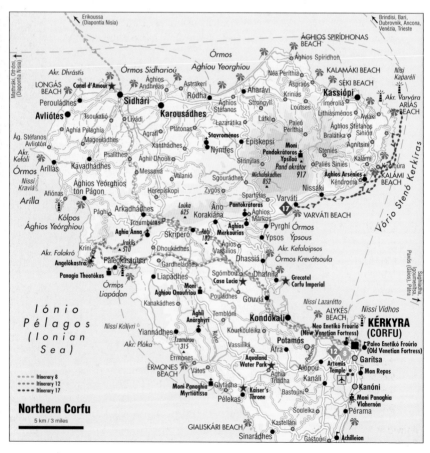

Northern Corfu

5 km / 3 miles

- - - Itinerary 8
- - - Itinerary 12
- - - Itinerary 17

set behind the Dhiapóndia islands. There's also a wide, sandy beach at **Ághios Stéfanos Avliotón**, 10km (6 miles) southwest of Sidhári, a package-tour centre where there are restaurants and rooms to let galore (*not* Ághios Stéfanos Sinión, covered on page 44). The northern end of this crescent-shaped beach is cleanest. Five minutes' walk west of the beach is a tiny caïque harbour; swimming off the rocks beyond the harbour beats braving the hordes on the beach in July.

The voyage to **Eríkoussa** (daily except Tues, departure 9.30am in high season; return 4pm) takes just under an hour. Of the three Dhiapóndia islets, Eríkoussa is the easternmost (Mathráki is furthest south and closest to Corfu, with a fabulous, long beach; Othoní is westernmost and is fairly inaccessible). Eríkoussa, where the former US President George Bush visited by helicopter, and Prince Charles by yacht, is as quiet as Corfu's northwest coast is noisy. Keeping an eye on your watch, set out on foot to ramble the island's peripheral roads: there's a simple map posted at the end of the jetty. Swimmers should seek out Bragíni beach, beyond Palaiokályva.

Garden Attractions

Eríkoussa is an underpopulated flower, fruit and vegetable garden, so just set out, and then return to the main beach (and port) to swim in clear waters before returning to Sidhári. The best place for lunch on the islet is the Hotel Erikoussa (tel/fax: 26630 71555/ 71110; May–mid-Sept, for all meals), but arrive early as when the food is gone, it's gone. The best time to photograph the Canal d'Amour is on the return voyage, when your captain will steer the boat close to the rocks, offering passengers the best photo opportunities.

Above: on the way to Eríkoussa
Right: a young passenger poses

9. ALONAKI BAY AND THE SOUTH *(see map, p49)*

This trip by hire car will take you further down Corfu's western coast, to stop at the Byzantine fortress of Gardhíki, swim off Halikoúnas Beach, view Lake Korissíon and lunch at secluded Alonáki Bay.

To the starting point: following the directions provided for Itinerary 13, proceed to the village of Sinarádhes, and then follow signs (to the right, just out of town) for Ághios Górdhis, which you reach after 3km (2 miles) of winding road. If you're going to do any walking, take sturdy shoes or hiking boots.

The western coastline is dramatic at **Ághios Górdhis**, but the beach is crowded in season, so head up and inland. After 2.5km (1½ miles) of steep and winding road, you enter the largely unspoilt farming village of Káto Garoúna. After a short distance, bear left towards Kérkyra and look out for a right turn towards Ághios Matthéos. In 3km (2 miles) you enter the village of Vouniatádhes, where every house has its own grape arbour. Some 2km (1¼ miles) further on, enter **Ághios Matthéos** and follow signs for Lefkími. This friendly, prosperous town has red-tiled buildings and a shady main street lined with cafés, should you wish to stop for a drink or an ice-cream.

About 1.5km (1 mile) from Ághios Matthéos, you'll come to a major group of signposts. Turn right for Halikoúnas and Gardhíki. After about

1km (½ mile), bear left and you will see the 13th-century Byzantine fortress of **Gardhíki** on your right. Get out and have a look inside the walls (watching out for snakes). The ruined walls here are divided into eight sections by postern towers and on an upper floor of the south tower, in what was once perhaps a chapel, are shadowy wall paintings of saints.

Drive for another 2km (1¼ miles), through silent groves, gardens and vineyards until you come to signs for Alonáki Bay, where you should bear right. The tarmac ends and the road turns to pebble, and you're entering a little corner of Corfu known only to the locals and a few visi-

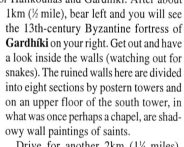

Above: pebbles from Halikoúnas Beach
Left: the Gardhíki fortress

tors. Some 2km (1¼ miles) further on, turn right at signs for **Alonáki Bay**. Here is a little taverna (tel: 26610 75872/76118; May–Oct, open all day, but phone in advance) serving local specialities – freshly caught fish, lobster and octopus, as well as shrimps from Lake Korissíon. Owned and run by Mihalis and Katerina Varagoulis and their family, the taverna comprises a few widely spaced tables sheltering beneath the low branches of stunted trees directly above the beach: heaven on earth. There are also a few rooms to let here if you feel like staying on.

Birdwatchers' Lake and Hideaway Beach

After lunch, retrace your route to the signs for Halikoúnas Beach. Turn right and proceed till the road turns to dirt. On your left, you will see the flat, blue waters of **Lake Korissíon**, of great interest to birdwatchers, who have identified some 150 species of birds on the island, among them the glossy ibis, spoonbill, pygmy cormorant and great white egret. On your right is **Halikoúnas Beach** – a secret haunt of the locals until now – with its expanse of shingle and strange, sculptural pebbles. Spread out your towel and have a swim on this largely deserted, silent stretch – a rare experience in the Ionian islands today.

   As you retrace your route to Kérkyra, less than 1km (just over ½ mile) back up the dirt track from Halikoúnas Beach you will notice the **Family**

Taverna Spyros (tel: 26610 76384) on the left. This little oasis of carefully tended flowers is a pleasant place to stop (it also has pristine toilet facilities). Mr and Mrs Spyros and Eleni Armeniakos cook for visitors as though they were family, and Eleni makes a delicious cup of Greek coffee: order it sweet *(glykós)* or medium *(métrios)*. You can stop just for a cold drink or an ice-cream as well. Suitably refreshed, continue on your way, bearing right into Ághios Matthéos and Sinarádhes, following clearly marked signs for the route back to Kérkyra.

10. ALTERNATIVE CORFU *(see map, p36)*

This little chapter introduces you to the Casa Lucia cottage complex and retreat, located outside the village of Sgómbou; Medi Jeunesse, in Kérkyra, which offers myriad skin treatments and fitness classes; and Ms Vana Soueref's beauty salon.

To the starting point: Casa Lucia is 12km (7½ miles) northwest of Kérkyra by taxi or rented car. About 11km (7 miles) from town, near the village of Sgómbou, you will turn left at a little blue sign for the cottage retreat, which is clearly signed, a short distance off the main road. Both Medi Jeunesse and Vana Soueref's salon are in or near the historic centre of Kérkyra.

In order to get to know a new culture well it is important to participate in the daily life of the foreign land just as you would at home, experiencing as much as you possibly can of what the culture has to offer on a day-to-day basis. So, between visits to the beach, explore alternative healing and meditation at Casa Lucia, take an aerobics class at Medi Jeunesse with young Greek instructors who speak very little English, and have Ms Vana Soueref style your hair – your stay will be so much the richer for it.

Casa Lucia (Sgómbou; tel: 26610 91419; fax: 26610 91732; e-mail: caslucia@otenet.gr; casa-lucia-corfu.com) was established by Mr and Mrs Dennis and Val Androutsopoulos in 1977. Today, the cottage complex comprises 11 bungalows, which are let out to visitors on a daily basis between Easter and the end of October, with maid service, swimming pool, wel-

come pack and other perks in high season; in winter, self-catering visitors may book accommodation by the week or the month.

Casa Lucia is a little paradise of meditative healing, the cottages set in a series of tailored gardens, but the remarkable facets of a stay here are the alternative healing and creative arts seminars, with sessions and workshops throughout the year. Do fax or e-mail Val direct, and she will supply you with a schedule of upcoming events. Book in advance if you want to visit in high season, though Val says that even if you show up unexpectedly, she often has a free cottage.

Your stay might coincide with a Tai Chi session and a mini-course in Sacred Circle dance. Other recent offerings have included a weekend-long Buddhist meditation retreat, Reiki at all three levels of mastery, shiatsu, aromatherapy, reflexology, acupuncture and herbal therapy treatments, Swedish massage, manicures and pedicures, and creative writing and poetry workshops.

At the end of a day at Casa Lucia, you may want to make the short drive to **Etrusco** (Káto Korakiána; tel: 26610 93342), one of Corfu's – and Greece's – most famous restaurants, to sample Chef Hector Bottrini's eclectic Italian cuisine. Call in advance for reservations, and, if you're planning to order from the 200-plus-label wine list, designate a driver for the journey home.

The Body Beautiful

Back in Kérkyra, there are other notable oases of pampering. Ms Areti Kourkoulou's **Medi Jeunesse** (16 Ioánni Andreádi Street; tel: 26610 43434/44475; also at 18 Spýrou Kondomári Street, off San Rócco Square; tel: 26610 25616/28030) offers fine skin treatments, as well as a plethora of fitness classes. Have your hotel desk book, say, a facial with Ms Kourkoulou herself, then proceed by taxi to her salon on San Rocco.

For women's and men's hair treatments – and outstanding cuts – Ms Vana Soueref's salon **Kommoteirio** (1 Delvinióti Street; tel: 26610 38362), located behind the old-town branch of the National Bank of Greece, is a pleasant place to have one's saltwater-stressed locks trimmed, shorn, styled, coloured or permed. Ms Soueref's English is minimal, which doesn't bother her international clientele in the least. Everyone goes out looking terrific! Have your hotel make your appointment in advance and explain exactly what services you want. (The reasonable prices for all aesthetic services on Corfu will be another nice surprise.)

Left: Tai Chi in motion
Above: Casa Lucia

11. Au Naturel at Myrtiotissa *(see map 33)*

This itinerary takes you by hire car to the island's only nudist beach, the heavenly Myrtiótissa, located roughly halfway down the island's gorgeous west coast.

To the starting point: set out from Kérkyra on the main Airport/Lefkími road, which you reach via the Garítsa Bay corniche, then follow route directions on page 53. Be sure to take sun protection with you: it is exposed in more ways than one on Myrtiótissa. Also, please note: the walk down to this beach, especially at midday in high season, is hot and challenging, and you will need to wear sturdy shoes. Small children and unfit visitors will probably find the descent difficult, and the ascent nearly impossible – and only those with a four-wheel-drive vehicle should attempt to drive close to the foot of the cliff.

Unlike Mykonos, where the majority of beaches are basically topless and/or have an accepted nudist end, Corfu has only one beach where nudity is tolerated, Myrtiótissa, and those looking for it have something of a wild goose chase ahead of them today. Once you have actually found Myrtiótissa, though, returning for a second visit is easy enough. It's that first time that's tricky, as signposting is at best primitive (hand-scrawled, nailed to trees, upside down, sometimes entirely non-existent). Maddeningly, the signs are actually posted just beyond the turns they indicate, an all-too-frequent phenomenon on the island. This route's as elusive as the Cheshire Cat, and having a navigator on board keeping his or her eyes peeled is an invaluable help for the driver.

Top: enjoying some shade
Above: subs on the beach

Getting There

Just past the airport, which is on your left, turn right for Pélekas, then almost immediately turn left. Proceed for about 10km (6 miles) on this road, passing the eyesore of the Aqualand Water Park on your left, then skirt the village of Ághios Ioánnis, before turning left for Érmones/Glyfáda. Make a note as you pass Aqualand of signs for the excellent French restaurant, **Spyros and Vasilis** – you may want to return here to dine later on during your stay (*see page 73*).

About 1.3km (¾ mile) further on, do not turn left for Kokkíni village proper, nor left for Pélekas/Sinarádhes – go straight on, following signs for Érmones. You will pass Camping Vátos on your left after some 2km (1¼ miles). Turn left at a sign saying Pélekas 5, Glyfáda 4: if you actually reach Érmones, you've gone 1km (½ mile) too far and will have to backtrack. If it's any consolation, absolutely everyone gets lost two or three times trying to locate Myrtiótissa.

After another 500m/yds or so, bear left at a hand-painted, all but invisible sign for Glyfáda, then almost immediately right down an abysmally signed road for Myrtiótissa which immediately turns to dirt and rather large stones. After another 500m/yds, park alongside other vehicles in a little goat-dotted olive grove. Continue on foot down a dirt and concrete road, which soon becomes steep and very rough, to Mr Spyros Kritikos's **Myrtiótissa Rooms** (tel: 26610 94113), a bar and restaurant where you can have a drink or lunch and catch your breath. There are also showers, hoses and toilet facilities here, which makes this a good place to stop after your swim.

A Shangri-La

Around 1km (½ mile) straight downhill from here is dramatic Myrtiótissa beach itself, which resembles a sort of Shangri-La after your arduous search

for the place. The sheer rock faces falling to the white sand and fresh water springs gushing from the rock itself – natural showers – make Myrtiótissa almost unbearably beautiful. On the beach you can rent umbrellas and sunbeds, shed your clothes and buy delicious, made-to-order submarine sandwiches and drinks at the cantina. The unpolluted water is clean, clear and teeming with little fish; the people who frequent this elusive place are almost uniformly friendly. Stay until the sun dips into the sea, and then wend your way up the hill in the relative cool of evening.

Return to town by retracing the route you took to get here. It's easier going back because everyone decamps at about the same time in the evening, and you can simply follow the traffic home.

Right: Myrtiótissa beach

12. THE ANGELOKASTRO AND PALEOKASTRITSA
(see map, p46)

This excursion by hire car takes you to the 12th-century castle of the Angelókastro, atop its dizzy precipice above the sea, near the village of Kríni; and to the beautiful, bustling resort town of Paleokastrítsa, where you visit the 13th-century Monastery of the Holy Virgin.

To the starting point: follow the same route as for Itinerary 8 (see page 45), as far as the village of Troumbétas, then follow directions below. Take along beach gear, but wear very modest clothing for your visit to the monastery – and you'll need sturdy walking shoes.

At Troumbétas, rather than head over the pass and down to the northwest littoral, follow signs for Alimatádhes and Vístonas. As you climb, you will

have dramatic views to the northwest and east, taking in the Dhiapóndia islets and Albania. Some 3km (2 miles) out of Troumbétas, go straight on, ignoring a sign on the right for Alimatádhes. The heights here are rich in grapes and olives and yellow with flowering broom in spring.

After 4.5km (3 miles), you pass through the village of Vístonas, with its olive oil presses and a delightful roadside stand called **The Mulberry Tree** (tel: 26630 49049). An Englishwoman called Joy runs this concern, along with her father-in-law, Mr Spyros Konstandis, as an outlet for the family's own range of wines, honey and olive oil, as well as hand-crafted lace and olive-wood bowls and implements.

Dramatic Vistas

As you head out of Vístonas, Angelókastro (Angel Castle) appears directly before you, looking for all the world like a Steven Spielberg special effect, floating on a pillar of olive trees: this is perhaps the single most dramatic sight on Corfu. Follow signs for Kríni and Angelókastro (and give souvenir-hawkers a wide berth as you enter Kríni: they will actually try to flag your car down to sell you things, a rarity in Greece).

Bear to the left and pass the Panorama Café. Continue, counter-intuitively downhill, following the frequent signs for the Angelókastro. The paved road winds through olive groves, netted for the harvest which takes place from late autumn to May. You will get a superb photo opportunity 1km (½ mile) out of Kríni: pull off the road into a small gravel lay-by to take stunning shots of the castle ahead. An equal distance downhill brings you to a car park and the ticket booth for the **Angelókastro** (now open again after restoration).

A Byzantine stronghold built for the 12th-century Emperor Manuel Komnenos, the castle proved to be an almost impregnable fortress and was known to the Angevins as the *Castrum Sancti Angeli*. It held out against attacks by pirates, the Genoese and the Ottoman Turkish invaders of Corfu, and was in use

Above: a gnarled olive tree

as a fortified retreat throughout the 16th century: some 300m (984ft) above the sea, with its own mighty water reservoir, Angelókastro's church was dedicated to the archangels Michael and Gabriel. (Watch attentively for snakes on your ascent to the summit: this fortress is still well guarded – but by reptiles.)

From the castle, you can see Kérkyra off in the distance to the southeast, and just about everything else in four directions. Retrace your route now to Makrádhes, where you will bear right for Lákones. Views down to the sea and the resort of Paleokastrítsa are breathtaking, but watch for oncoming traffic. The Bella Vista Grill/Bar or the Golden Fox on the road here are good places to stop, take refreshment, and savour the view. **Lákones**, which you reach after 1km (½ mile) or so, is a roadside village where elderly women in traditional, white Corfiot headscarves sit on their doorsteps and watch the passing parade. Descend sharply, then, through terraced olive groves, following signs for Paleokastrítsa.

A Monastic Haven

Paleokastrítsa, one of the island's most famous resorts, is lively and loud in high season, the traffic all but eclipsing the natural beauty of the place, which comprises dramatic azure coves, verdant promontories and intimate beaches. One area of Paleokastrítsa which retains all its beauty is the 13th-century **Monastery of the Holy Virgin** (daily 7am–1pm, 3–8pm), with its remarkable church. Home to a handful of monks and novices, some from Central Europe, this fortified eyrie has a stunning church containing icons of the Virgin to which miracles have been attributed, and a beautiful, painted, mid-18th-century iconostasis, or icon screen. The monastery gardens are verdant and peaceful and a little museum exhibits 16th- and 17th-century vestments, icons and the skeleton of what residents describe as a 'sea monster', actually an unfortunate whale which was slaughtered in

Above: dramatic Angelókastro
Right: Kríni villagers take a view on life

1860 by French seamen. The monastery and resort celebrate three feast days – on the first Friday after Orthodox Easter, on 13 July and on 15 August – at which times it's standing room only in Paleokastrítsa.

Adjacent to the monastery is an unnamed restaurant – more a café, really – that makes a hospitable venue for light meals, snacks and drinks, all consumed among the perambulating monastery peacocks (which can never be coaxed into spreading their kaleidoscopic tails). Alternatively, on the way back out of town, at the foot of steps leading down to the sea, is the **Akron Beach Bar and Tennis Court** (tel: 26630 41226), a good place to combine lunch and/or dinner with a swim and a pricy but worthwhile trip by hired motor boat to nearby, but almost inaccessible, beaches. Mpre committed visitors can patronise one of three local scuba schools offering dives into the brisk water here.

13. FOLKLORE HERITAGE OF CORFU *(see map, p33)*

Set aside a Thursday to visit Sinarádhes folklore museum; spend the evening with dinner or just drinks by the pool at the Grecotel Corfu Imperial in Komméno, for a performance of authentic Greek dancing.

To the starting point: leave Kérkyra via the airport/Lefkími road. After less than 1km (½ mile), follow signs right for Pélekas. The road passes through Alepoú and Tríklino, where you'll see a sign for Pélekas 7km (4¼ miles). Bear left for Pélekas/Sinarádes. In about 3km (2 miles), you'll come to a crossroads. Turn left for Sinarádes (sign in Greek only) and, immediately, you're in the village.

In **Sinarádhes**, park near the little town square, with its lone central palm tree, and walk slightly uphill. Across from the Philharmonic Society of Sinarádhes and the Church of Ághios Nikólaos, signs to the museum will direct you up steps. Wend your way steeply uphill and left and in a short distance you will reach the **Folklore Museum of Central Corfu** (daily 9.30am–2.30pm, closed Sun and Mon; entrance fee).

The house here is typical of rural central Corfu, and dates from 1860, but since life on the island changed little over the following century the lifestyle mirrored here could just as easily represent Corfu in 1960, when your author first visited the island. The simplicity – and poverty – of life for most Corfiots up until very recent times is evocatively expressed in the Spartan nature of this dwelling.

As you enter the first-floor living quarters (the ground floor is still a private residence), you see a *pithári*, which would have contained the family's year-long supply of olive oil, the staple of the Greek diet then as now. An entire family would have lived in these three sparsely furnished rooms – perhaps 10 people, who would have been out in the fields all day, coming home to roost only at night. Most rural life went on out of doors, and dwellings were simply a place for eating and sleeping.

The exhibits are well marked in English and German, and helpful staff members will tell you much about the artefacts. The kitchen, a bedroom and a 'formal' parlour or dining room (opened only for special occasions such as saints' days and engagements), comprise the home. Notice the traditional birthing chair, a type still used by some local midwives. Upstairs – where a second family would have lived – is a display of some interesting non-domestic exhibits: a primitive papyrus boat, used on the west coast of Corfu until the mid-20th century (and of a type dating back to the Egyptians); a loom; agricultural tools; a shadow puppet *(karaghiózis)* theatre; a cobbler's bench; and a potter's wheel. There's also an exhibit on Corfiot women's headscarves, each of which would have denoted the wearer's village of origin and her marital status, simply through colour and pattern.

After viewing the museum, wander around Sinarádhes for a while, to discover a farming village that still remains much as it was in 1860.

Folk Dance Evenings

Drive back to your hotel in the afternoon, have a siesta perhaps, and then don your finery and head out to Komméno and the **Grecotel Corfu Imperial** (tel: 26610 91481/2; performances Thurs 8–11.30pm, Sun 9–11.30pm). This complex, which sprawls beautifully over much of the Komméno peninsula, with spectacular gardens and superb bars and restaurants, comprises the island's finest hotel. You can sit by the pool, sip a Bellini or a beer from either the Alkinoos or Odysseus bar, and watch (or join in with) the professional troupe of trad- itionally costumed Greek dancers, and there's a barbecue dinner to accompany the dancing. (If you prefer your music cool, there's usually a duo playing indoors at the Art Deco-styled Alkinoos Bar.)

Left: traditional home in Sinarádhes. **Above:** Corfiot dancers

The Odysseus Bar has an impressive cocktail menu, including something called a Grecotel Surprise in the heat of summer: 3 parts gin, 2 parts exotic fruit liqueur, 1 part Amaretto, with orange juice and strawberry syrup to fill. (Good thing you're not driving back to your lodgings.) There's also draught Mythos and Warsteiner Pils, champagne cocktails galore and Piper Heidsieck by the glass, all reasonably priced, considering this is a luxury complex.

If you prefer to dine elsewhere (and there is no hotel barbecue on Sunday), you will still have time to do this after the show. Consult the *Eating Out* section of this guide, and reserve a table for late evening. Spyros and Vasilis, or Etrusco would be good nearby choices *(see pages 72–3)*.

14. SUNDAY IN KERKYRA *(see map, p20–1)*

Start the day in Kérkyra with a church service at the Holy Trinity Angli-can Church, then take a tour of the British Cemetery, preferably in the company of Hilary Whitton Païpeti, a noted local writer and guide. Spend the evening at two quintessentially Corfiot night spots – the cin-ema and the New Fortress's Morrison Café, which is located within the Venetian battlements.

To the starting point: if you want your visit to the cemetery to include the guided tour, contact Ms Païpeti (PO Box 445, Kérkyra, Corfu, 49100 Greece; tel/fax: 26610 52833; e-mail: corfiotm@otenet.gr) well in advance to make arrangements. Holy Trinity Church is just two or three blocks west of the Spi-anádha, a stone's throw from the Bella Venezia Hotel.

In 1864, when the British Protectorate (which is what the British occu-pation of Corfu was called) ended, and the Church of St George within the Old Fortress became Greek Orthodox, the Greek authorities offered the Ionian Parliament building 'to the Corfu community of the Anglican faith'. Today, **Holy Trinity Anglican Church** (21 L Mavíli Street; tel: 26610 31467; service Sun at 10.30am, 1st and 3rd Sun 7pm) is spiritual home to a diverse body of Corfiot, expatriate and visiting Christians, of all denom-inations and nationalities. On a recent Pentecost, Alba-nian, American, British, Canadian, Dutch, Filipino, German, Greek, Irish, Mexican, North Ethiopian, South African and Swiss worshippers were in attendance. Reg-ular services are conducted by the Reverend Clifford Owen (of Staffordshire) – and Holy Communion on Sunday morn-ings is followed by refreshments in the garden. At 7pm, every other Sunday, an informal Songs of Praise service is held. A little book, written by parishioners and entitled *A Faith Odyssey*, is available in the church office.

Roman Catholic services are held at the **Roman Catholic Cathedral** or **Duomo of Ágios Iákovos** (Platía Dhimarhíou; May–Sept, Sat 7pm, Sun 8.30am, 10am and 7pm), and there are other Catholic services at Gozzela, in Dhassiá, and at the Catholic Camping in Messongí; check at the Duomo for hours.

Above: serving the spiritual needs of some of Corfu's expatriates
Right: the British cemetery

itineraries

Garden of Peace and Poetry

After church, take a taxi to Kolokotróni Street, the location of the lovely **Anglikó Nekrotafío** (British Cemetery), which dates from the years of the British Protectorate (1814–64). You don't have to take a guided tour, but it is highly recommended because Hilary Whitton Païpeti's knowledge adds so much to the experience. (You may also be interested to know that Ms Païpeti leads a variety of tours on the island, including Corfiot Wildflowers in Spring, The Durrell Tour, Picturesque Corfiot Villages and Corfiot Fortresses.) A garden full of 'English poetry' and peace on a verdant hill above the town, the cemetery has a dazzling array of Corfiot flora, both wild and cultivated, which is at its best in April or May. Botanists and gardeners from all over the world visit the British Cemetery in spring to examine over 45 types of wild orchid that bloom here.

The monuments and gravestones within these walls tell the whole history of the British on Corfu, and military historians will be fascinated by the eloquent markers dating from both world wars. As remarkable as the wildflowers and the stones is the cemetery's caretaker, Mr George Psaïlas, who was actually born and married in the cemetery, and who has already prepared his own grave and marker. A fount of information about the 'residents' of his garden, Mr Psaïlas is a sort of Corfiot historian-philosopher. Share a few moments with him in his backyard, so to speak, and wander among the evocative stones. (Mr Psaïlas is also something of a writer: ask to purchase his pair of little booklets on the cemetery and its orchids.)

When you've seen enough, turn right out of the front gate and, at the end of the block, right again into Mitropolíti Methodhíou Street. Proceed four blocks downhill to San Rocco Square. As Ms Païpeti tells her charges, this street is lined with 'real' Greek shops – hardware, hairdressers and plumbers – so you get a glimpse of Kérkyra life away from the touristic centre. On Sunday many of these workaday emporia will be closed, but shops catering for tourists, as well as cafés and restaurants, will all be open.

The Commercial Heart of Town

San Rocco Square, the 17th-century marketplace that developed outside the main gate to the old Venetian city, the Porto Reale, is noisy and congested but it's where most of the town's business takes place and where the blue-bus terminal and a taxi rank are located. Cross Alexándhras Avenue here, and go straight ahead on Yeorghíou Theotóki Street, the main modern shopping thoroughfare. Proceed three blocks further on, passing Marks & Spencer (the original location of the Porto Reale), and entering the old town near the National Bank of Greece. The Roman Catholic church here was demolished by a German bombardment during World War II.

The road changes names here, becoming Vlahióti Street. Turn left at the fountain, in a square known locally as the Piazza, into Mihaïl Theotóki Street. At the end of a short block, turn right into Nikifórou Theotóki Street and proceed east to Kapodhistríou Street and the familiar territory of the Listón. If you are hungry, the Aegli or the Rex are nearby, but you may want to return to your lodgings to freshen up, then find a place for an early dinner.

Take a taxi unless you are within walking distance, to the corner of Yerásimou Aspióti and Akadhimías streets; you may wish to pause here and spray on some mosquito repellent. Here, right in the heart of town is the summer cinema Phoenix (not to be confused with the winter cinema Orfeas, also located near here), one of the most popular warm-weather, after-dark venues for the locals.

Movies under the Stars

The **Summer Cinema Phoenix** (Fínikas; 1 Ioánnou Daliétou Street; tel: 26610 37482; early Jun–early Sept, 9.30pm–midnight), a 250-seat open-air cinema within a walled garden, shows recent Greek and foreign films in a festive setting. You can order pizza to be delivered here, or simply buy snacks, beer and soft drinks at the bar. And don't be choosy about what film is showing on the night you attend. It's the entire experience of watching a film under a sparkling Corfiot sky while sipping a cold Mythos beer that is so special – even if it is a B-movie that you'd never dream of watching back home.

From mid-Sept–May, Corfiot movie-goers repair to the indoor **Winter Cinema Orfeas** (tel: 26610 39768; tickets around €7) nearby on Yerásimou Aspióti. When the film finishes at about 11pm, intrepid night-owls may choose to ascend to the New Fortress, small flashlights in hand. Within the Venetian battlements, the **Morrison Café** (tel: 26610 27477), run by Argyris and George Dimitrakis, rocks till dawn. Friday and Saturday nights, even in winter, you're likely to find performances of eclectic, live music here.

Above: stringing garlic

15. WESTERN BEACHES AND SPORT *(see map, p33)*

This hire car itinerary takes you on a strictly hedonistic tour of some of the west coast's beautiful beaches. You could take time out to walk a section of the Corfu Trail or for a round of golf at the Corfu Golf Club.

To the starting point: if you want to play golf (choose 9 holes for time on the beach too), call the Corfu Golf Club (tel: 26610 94220) well in advance to reserve your tee time and club hire. The same applies to walking part of the Corfu Trail in the Ropa Valley: contact Aperghi Travel (tel: 26610 48713; fax: 26610 48715) in advance for informaion. Follow the directions for Itinerary 11 (see page 52), until you get just beyond the village of Kokkíni. Take bathing gear for the beach and sun protection for any of the day's activities.

Just beyond Kokkíni, following signs for the Louis Grand Hotel, turn left off the main road down to **Glyfádha Beach**. This is a long, long stretch of developed, but not ruined beachfront, dramatically situated and isolated by sheer vertical cliffs that plunge to the sea – and there is real surf here when the offshore wind is blowing hard. Watersports galore, sunbeds and umbrellas are on offer on the beach, and the crowd is fun-loving and young. There's an enormous car park at the foot of the cliffs. If you find that you like Glyfádha enough to return sometime for a longer stay, there are apartments and time-shared condominiums at **Menigos Beach Resort** (Glyfádha/Pélekas, Corfu, 49100 Greece; tel: 26610 95074, fax 26610 94933*), an attractive place to stay, right on the beach; contact them well in advance of your visit. Have lunch at the **Agnes Restaurant** (tel: 26610 94231) halfway down the beach, where Agnes cooks simple Greek fare in her small kitchen.

Above: Glyfádha beach
Right: lunch at Agnes Restaurant

A Scenic Golfing Challenge

After a swim, retrace your route uphill to the Kokkíni/Érmones road, turn left and after 1km (½ mile), you will come to the **Corfu Golf Club** (near Érmones; tel/fax: 26610 94220), located in the idyllic, fertile Rópa Valley. Designed by Swiss-based course architect Donald Harradine, the 18-hole, Par 72-SSS 72 course blends the challenges and beauties of the valley's natural terrain with man-made hazards. Featuring lakes, streams and copses of indigenous trees, the picturesque greens are among the Mediterranean's best-kept secrets, but the club has many visiting players who come back time and again for the scenery, the quirky challenge of golfing in Greece, and the sheer pleasure of the laid-back atmosphere in the impressive clubhouse. Golfers and their families will enjoy the facilities here. There's the inevitable pro shop with bags and clubs for hire (and club shirts for sale), a bar and lounge with satellite television and pool tables, a clubhouse restaurant which is open all day for snacks as well as full meals, and there are showers and changing facilities where you can freshen up.

Mr Hunt offers various lessons ranging from 30- to 60-minute sessions and 9-holes tuition (for individuals or groups of two or three golfers) to courses of six lessons. Green fees (subject to change) start at €47 for 18 holes, but if you want to play every day for a week, this goes down to €30 a day, with an eighth day thrown in for free. Hiring golf cars, trolleys, clubs and driving range balls is extra, and you must book in advance.

Walking The Corfu Trail

The Corfu Trail, a vast network of footpaths, clearly marked with yellow signs reading CT, and taking in, en route, all the island's natural wonders, upland villages and historic sites, north to south, is the labour of love of longtime Corfiot resident, British writer Hilary Whitton Païpeti. If you want

itineraries

to follow part of the CT itinerary – the Ropa Valley to the Angelókastro, for example – contact Aperghi Travel ahead of time or visit www. traveling.gr/corfutrail. Armed with sunblock, hat and sturdy footwear, you can take in a stretch of the trail, from the lush Ropa Valley to the medieval heights of the Angelókastro. For trekking enthusiasts, the entire trail comprises 250km (155 miles), and may be undertaken in 8 to 12 days *(see page 96 for Whitton Païpeti's guides to the trail, including detailed maps)*.

Sunset over Pélekas

Beyond the golf course and riding stables, you can continue for 1km (just over ½ mile) to the **Érmones Beach** community. Here, you can take a small boat to Apelístra and Andipsós beachlets, accessible only by sea. There's a scuba diving school below the vast Sunmarotel complex (and it's fun to ride the *téléferique* up to the hotel, with its grand view and huge swimming pool). The no-frills Nafsika taverna, on a hill overlooking the beach, is a good spot for coffee or cold drinks.

Below **Pélekas**, on your way back to Kérkyra, you will pass signs for Pélekas beach and Yialiskári beach: the first large and fairly developed, the latter smaller and more dramatically situated, with a quiet snack bar on the beach. If you happen to be near Pélekas around sunset on a summer's evening, take to the heights above the village, and seek out Kaiser Wilhelm II's well-signed little aerie-with-a-telescope. Popularly known as 'the Kaiser's Throne', this is one of the best (and, in high season, one of the busiest) places on the west coast from which to view the sunset, and, panoramically, the entire east coast of the island. The Levant Hotel, perched atop vertically rising Pélekas village, is a good place for coffee and ice-cream.

16. THE WILD, WOOLLY EAST *(see map, p49)*

This itinerary takes you down the heavily developed east coast, through the busy seaside resort of Benítses, then inland and up into the hills to pastoral Hlomós, dipping down finally to wild and woolly Kávos.

To the starting point: pick up a hire car and leave Kérkyra via the main Airport/Lefkími road.

Bear left following signs for Benítses and Lefkími, and 6km (4 miles) out of town, on your left, you will see the little peninsula of Kanóni, the monastery and church of Panaghía Vlahernón, and Pondikoníssi *(see pages 35 and 37)*. Some 9km (5½ miles) after leaving Kérkyra, you will see on your left

Left: walking the Corfu Trail
Above: Nafsika taverna

what is left of **Kaiser Wilhelm II's Bridge**, actually the stone jetty where the royal yacht, the *Hohenzollern*, put in. If you want to have a closer look – and the place is as romantic as a film set – be careful how and where you park. This is an extremely dangerous stretch of very narrow road.

The coast road south hugs the sea and in another 1km (½ mile), you enter the beach resort of **Benítses**. You'll need the patience of Job to get through town in high season but you can see, in this former fishing village, the lineaments of lost beauty and the effect upon it of mass tourism. Benítses segues seamlessly into Melitíes, and in another 6km (4 miles), you pass through a tunnel and enter **Ághios Ioánnis Peristerón** with its little family-oriented beach. About 3km (2 miles) further on you come to busy Moraïtika, and shortly bear right and inland, following signs for Lefkími.

A Traditional Upland Village

In about 7km (4¼ miles), you will pass through the village of Línia, where you turn left for the upland hamlet of **Hlomós**, 3km (2 miles) further. The terraced olive groves and views down to Lake Korissíon are a welcome anti-

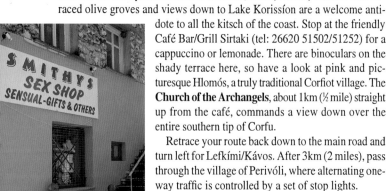

dote to all the kitsch of the coast. Stop at the friendly Café Bar/Grill Sirtaki (tel: 26620 51502/51252) for a cappuccino or lemonade. There are binoculars on the shady terrace here, so have a look at pink and picturesque Hlomós, a truly traditional Corfiot village. The **Church of the Archangels**, about 1km (½ mile) straight up from the café, commands a view down over the entire southern tip of Corfu.

Retrace your route back down to the main road and turn left for Lefkími/Kávos. After 3km (2 miles), pass through the village of Perivóli, where alternating one-way traffic is controlled by a set of stop lights.

Above: the Church of the Archangels, Hlomós
Left: sex sells in Kávos

'Sun and Sex' Tourism

Bypass Lefkími – the large, workaday 'Capital of the South', bisected by a canal-like river – past which it's another 8km (5 miles) southeast, to **Kávos**. There are no signs in Greek here, but a plethora of hoardings for venues that promise combinations of sex, alcohol and fun. In addition, the main bar strip through town is dotted with many 'surgeries' heralded by big red crosses and assurances of 24-hour service – an indication of just how festive it gets here after dark. In summer, groups of northern European youths, five or six abreast – shaven headed, tattooed and inebriated – swing through the streets even at noon. Groups of young northern European girls – blonde, tattooed, equally inebriated – follow.

The Corfiot authorities have pretty well 'quarantined' what they see as undesirable tourism to Kávos: young package tourists are transferred in from the airport, deposited at prepaid rooms, and then collected at the week's end and redeposited at the airport. In the interim, during high season, Kávos – with its widescreen TVs, forever tuned to British sports channels, and its busy bars and surgeries – is theirs.

17. NORTHEAST COAST BY CAIQUE *(see map, p46)*

This boat trip by traditional fishing caïque takes in the stunning, and largely empty, small beaches and coves of the northeast coast of the island. A swim at secluded Ariás Beach, lunch at Ághios Stéfanos Sinión and Lawrence Durrell's White House at Kalámi are added pleasures. A suggested alternative lets you explore the coast from under the water.

To the starting point: a day or two in advance, call Mr Ioakeim 'Iakis' Sgouros (tel: 69324 52739), to book the trip, and ask about fees and the particular itineraries he has available during your stay. Take a bus or preferably hire a car for the journey to meet the Vivi *at either Barbáti, Glýfa or Nissáki beaches (though other starting points, such as the resort of Ýpsos, are also negotiable).*

There are many scheduled excursions by boat up and down the coast of Corfu, but the day and evening cruises aboard the traditional little fishing caïque, the *Vivi*, with her captain, Mr Iakis Sgouros, are the most pleasant way to see Corfu from the sea. The *Vivi* is a 9-m (29-ft) long traditional Corfiot fishing craft, fully refitted for passengers, and her seaman-by-summer and master-stonemason-by-winter skipper, Iakis (married to an English woman, Vanessa, who comes from Salisbury) is a delightful and knowledgeable guide who makes certain his small group of passengers (usually some five to 15 foreign visitors) have a safe and lovely voyage.

The *Vivi* has several regular itineraries, but the most spectacular is the day-long excursion up the

Right: get on board the *Vivi*

northeast coast (Mon, Wed, Fri, approximately 10.30am–5pm). For an extremely reasonable fare, exclusive of snacks and meals ashore (which are also reasonably priced), you will have an experience of the island that is not possible via wheeled transport: the coves and tiny, pristine beaches called at by the *Vivi* are only accessible from the sea. Don't forget to take along sunhats and sunglasses, sunblock, beach towels, bathing costumes, swimming shoes (for protection against sea urchins) and pre-frozen bottles of drinking water.

Durrell's Swimming Place

Iakis picks up his passengers at two or three prearranged rendezvous points, then heads lazily up the northeast coast, stopping at tiny coves en route to show you marine caves and the tiny seaside **Chapel of Ághios Arsénios**, perched atop picturesquely buckling sedimentary strata. The sea here is azure and pristine, and the rocky coast is just incredibly beautiful. It was at Ághios Arsénios that novelist Lawrence Durrell and his wife once dropped cherries into the clear waters. This was, with good reason, the British author's favourite bathing spot on Corfu.

At **Kouloúra**, Iakis will usually break out the ouzo and fruit juice for one and all. On the coast here, too, your captain will point out the villas that belong to the rich and famous – the late Gianni Agnelli (of Fiat) had a residence here, as Jacob Rothschild still does. The straits between Corfu and Albania now narrow dramatically and the *Vivi* is frequently passed by Greek Coast Guard vessels patrolling the waterway.

Further north, you drop anchor at **Ariás Beach**, deserted except for the day-visiting pleasure craft and their passengers, and have a swim in the transparent waters. If you have a snorkel and mask, it's fun to explore underwater here, but watch out for the occasional sea urchin.

After your swim, Iakis will head back to **Ághios Stéfanos Sinión**, and stop an hour or so here while you have lunch and sunbathe on the beach. He usually drops you at the **Taverna Galini** (tel: 26630 81492), where the best choices on the menu are fresh fish or a fresh pork *brizola* (chop), drenched in oregano and lemon juice. Good local wines are available here, too.

After another half hour or so at sea, the *Vivi* again anchors at **Kalámi Bay**. Lawrence Durrell once made his home here in the **White House**, which today comprises rooms for rent upstairs and a good restaurant downstairs. Peek inside at photos and framed clippings about Kalámi's most famous former resident, and have a cup of Greek coffee or an ice-cream on the café terrace overlooking the sea. From here, at about 5pm, it's back to your point of embarkation.

Above: the Chapel of Ághios Arsénios
Top Right: the *Vivi* moors. **Right:** taking a look over the side

It is possible to take other trips on the *Vivi*. On Tuesday, Thursday and Saturday Iakis takes passengers south, again from Barbáti or Glyfádha, to Kérkyra for shopping and sightseeing, and to Vídhos islet for a swim. On Sunday, in season, there's a special 'Fresh Fish Barbecue Cruise' and, twice a week, romantic 'Sunset Cruises' to secluded beach tavernas.

Underwater Corfu

Another way of experiencing Corfu's fabulous east coast is underwater with a scuba tank. Arrange a scuba diving excursion in advance with Mr Christos Mourikis of the **Professional Diving Center** (2 Ioánnou Gardhikióti Street, Gouviá Marina; tel: 26610 91955; mobile: 69369 36790; fax: 26610 26909; www.diveincorfu.gr), located within the Marina at Gouviá. Mr Mourikis offers dives and diving courses of all kinds – and is not averse to taking the occasional snorkeller out on his boat as well. If you're not certified as a scuba diver and want just a splash of underwater Corfu, you may opt for the centre's 'one-day, one-dive' option, accompanied by a professional scuba diving instructor. A wide selection of other courses is also available here. At whatever level of proficiency you choose to enter Corfu's underwater world you will take away indelible memories of this island.

If you're interested in chartering a yacht, next door to the Professional Diving Center, you will find Vassilis and Anna Vrakotas's **Vrakotas Yachting Ltd**, under the 'Moorings' banners (PO Box 15, Corfu 49100; tel: 26610 99475; fax 26610 99476; e-mail: vyachts@otnet.gr; www.vrakotasyachting.com). Mr Vrakotas can arrange 10–16-m (32–54-ft) yachts and motorboats, bare-boat and skippered. **Gouvia Marina** is a full-service facility serving every imaginable need (PO Box 60, 49083, Tzavros, Corfu; tel: 26610 91900/91376; fax: 26610 91829; e-mail: gouvia@medmarinas.com; www.medmarinas.com).

Leisure Activities

SHOPPING

No one is supposed to visit Corfu without purchasing a bottle of the island's famous (infamous? violently chartreuse? undrinkable?) kumquat liqueur or, alternatively, candied kumquats in a decorative glass container. If traditional Greek foodstuffs and sweets packaged as gifts, museum-quality copies of Byzantine jewels, or limited edition bronze sculptures by Greece's foremost artists are more what you had in mind, there are some interesting shops you will want to seek out.

With your map of the town centre in hand, and the following list of shops, you will be able to locate and peruse the best of what the island has to offer in the way of tangible treasures. But it can also be fun just losing yourself in the bazaar that is the historic centre. Chock-a-block with shops of all sorts, it's a labyrinth of delights. Shops are open Monday, Wednesday, Saturday, 9am–2.30pm; Tuesday, Thursday, Friday, 9am–2pm and 6–9pm.

Speciality Shops
Art and Crafts
Fos tis Anatolis (or Ex Oriente Lux)
8 Kapodhistríou Street, Upper Spianádha, Kérkyra
Tel: 26610 45273/45259
This appealing emporium of pricy, quality Greek gifts, located in a lovely historic building, stocks jewellery and worry beads in silver and semi-precious stones, handknotted carpets, blown glass, ceramics, picture frames and essential oils derived from Greek flowers and herbs.

...kai to plío févghi! ('...and the ship departs!')
109 Nikifórou Theotóki Street, Kérkyra
Tel: 26610 39068
Mr Kostas Romantzis's shop is filled with nostalgic and whimsical Greek jewellery, sophisticated wooden mechanical toys, small

limited edition sculptures and ships made from olive wood.

Leather Forum
1 Par. Nikifórou Theotóki Street, Kérkyra
Tel: 26610 35963
With two locations in Kérkyra's town center, this family-run business is the place to go for leather handbags, briefcases, wallets, belts and luggage.

Olive Wood Handmade
76 Nikifórou Theotóki Street, Kérkyra
(no phone)
Get yourself a practical and attractive souvenir or gift: locally made bowls or cutting boards in olive wood. If oiled regularly and made from a single block of wood (rather than glued pieces), they will last for years.

Opsi
44 Filarmonikís, Kérkyra
Tel: 26610 41429
French expat Mireille Falquet, assisted by her mutt, Alítis ('Ruffian'), runs this eclectic gift-shop-cum-gallery. She stocks small sculptures in ceramics and bronze, Aphrodite Goulas's contemporary jewellery and copies of ancient Greek toys, etc.

Terracotta: Contemporary Greek Art
2 Filarmonikís Street, Kérkyra
Tel: 26610 45260
This small gallery exhibits works in bronze, precious metals, stone and clay by some 25

Left: fruit afloat
Right: crafted in Paxiot olive-wood

contemporary Greek artists and jewellers. Don't miss Thodoros Papagianni's sculptures; Mary Margoni's distinctive silver and gold rings set with large semi-precious stones; and large ceramic wall-hangings of butterflies by Keti Anastasaki.

Books and Music
Lykoudhis Bookstore
4 Vrokini Street , Kérkyra
Tel: 26610 39845
This bookshop and stationer's has served the public for 40 years. Lykoudhis also stocks a wide selection of foreign-language books and maps on Corfu.

Melpo G. Tourmousoglou
47 Nikifórou Theotóki Street
Tel: 26610 38451
Open till midnight in summer, Melpo and her son, Yiorgos, carry foreign press, magazines, and maps, and a good selection of guide books on Greece.

Mouses (Muses) Record Shop
9 and 22 Mihaïl Theotóki Street, Kérkyra
Tel: 26610 30708/37954/36994
A floor-to-ceiling, wall-to-wall treasure trove of both Greek and imported CDs, and a great place to procure 'audible memories' of your Corfiot sojourn. Ask owner Takis Alexandrou for help: his shop is about the best in Greece for breadth of selection and friendly service.

Food and Drink
Andriotis Traditional Patisserie & Cake Shop
1 Maniarízi keh Arlióti Street
(Kandoúni Bízi), Kérkyra
Tel: 26610 38045/38013
This is a no-frills, family-run and superlative Greek sweet shop with variations on Corfu's sugary kumquat theme and traditional Greek confections of all sorts.

Kava Païpeti
7 Maniarízi keh Arlióti Street (Kandoúni Bízi), Kérkyra
Tel: 26610 30778/26620
There is kumquat liqueur or whole kumquats in syrup in quantity here, but this *kava* (wine cellar/off license) is really noted for its phenomenal selection of fine wine – Greek (from some 400 wineries), French and Italian.

Starenio
51 Guílford Street, Kérkyra
Tel: 26610 47370
Friendly Nikos and Anna Kondopoulos run this emporium of baked goods, sweets and traditional Greek foodstuffs – a treat for the eye, nose and taste buds. There's *mandoláto* (almond nougat), *mandóles* (burnt sugared almonds), Corfiot biscuits of all sorts, a cornucopia of breads (garlic, olive, olive oil, corn, honey and sunflower seed, honey and walnut) and traditional Greek pastries.

Jewellery
Folli Follie
32 Mihaïl Theotóki Street, Kérkyra
Tel: 26610 30743
This classy Greek chain features fashion jewellery and accessories – all modern, sleek and wearable.

Ilias Lalaounis
35 Kapodhistríou Street, Kérkyra
Tel: 26610 36258
Greece's 'ambassadors of gold', Mr Ilias Lalaounis and his family, have put the

country firmly on the international map as far as gold jewellery is concerned. With many locations throughout Greece and the world, Lalaounis's designs in gold, semi-precious and precious stones are always fresh, creative, impeccably finished and, unlike much Greek gold, light enough to wear comfortably.

Mag

36 Nikifórou Theotóki Street, Kérkyra
Tel: 26610 43580

Mr and Mrs Michael and Elsi Agistriotis's Mag (a Belgian-Greek jewellery concern with other shops on Corfu, in mainland Greece and Antwerp) features a wealth of sophisticated gold and silver jewellery. Especially beautiful are Mag's interpretations of Greek Byzantine pieces in gold and precious stones, created by hand using ancient skills.

Miscellaneous
English Imports

1st Párodhos Mitropolíti Methodhíou Street, off San Rocco Square, Kérkyra
Tel: 26610 47692

One of the permanent foreign community's favourite haunts, this little shop carries UK chain store goods, linens, clothing, gift items, periodicals and books. (Look for author Hilary Whitton-Païpeti's books, especially.) Run by Susan, Jane and Diana, the store features a bulletin board listing a treasure trove of local information.

Mandala

16 Sevastianoú Street, Kérkyra
Tel: 26610 32705

Mr Friderikos Avgerinos visits India and Nepal each year, off season, and buys stock for his distinctive shop – textiles, statuary, clothing, jewellery and accessories. It's a lovely little oasis just off the Listón. (Turn off Kapodhistríou Street into Sevastíanoú at the Häagen-Dazs ice-cream shop.)

Tobacconists/Newsagents/ Photographic Supplies
Kiosk

11 Kapodhistríou Street and 9 Velissaríou Street, Kérkyra
Tel: 26610 42760

Operated by the Grammenos family, these newsagents and tobacconists have a stag-gering array of newspapers and periodicals especially foreign-language, plus cigarettes and cigars, including Havanas.

Photo Fast Liston

11/A Kapodhistríou Street, behind the Listón, Kérkyra
Tel: 26610 21629

Photographer Yiannis Vlachos and his colleagues will get your prints back to you in under an hour, but this little shop also carries camera supplies and film in a convenient location.

Photo Tabac Ghitsis

52 Nikifórou Theotóki Street, Kérkyra
Tel: 26610 32005

Kostas Ghitsis's chock-a-block hole-in-the-wall has everything you could need in terms of tobacco, Cuban cigars, collectible toys, camera equipment, batteries, portable electronic equipment, etc. Open 7.30am till midnight in summer.

For those looking for a little slice of home-from-home shopping – though be aware that clothing stocks are tweaked to fit local tastes – the following listings in Kérkyra may be of interest: **The Body Shop**, tel: 26610 26539, 13 Platía Iróön Kypriakoú Agóna; **Marks & Spencer**, tel: 26610 41360, 15–17 Yeorghíou Theotóki Street; and **Benetton**, tel: 26610 23900, 9 Platía Iróön Kypriakoú Agóna.

EATING OUT

The Food of Corfu
by Diana Farr Louis

Corfiot cooking is quintessentially Mediter-ranean: laced with sweet virgin olive oil bal-anced with the acidity of tomatoes and lemon juice, heady with garlic and reliant on herbs like basil, mint and parsley for taste. Occa-sionally the Corfiots – alone among the Ionian islanders – spice their food with paprika, both hot and sweet, a habit whose origin is still debated.

Unlike most of the rest of Greece, Corfu was never occupied by the Ottoman Turks. Instead, its cuisine, like its architecture, reflects the lengthy presence of the Vene-tians and, to a lesser extent, the British. On

Left: kumquats come in many guises

many menus you'll find dishes with deceptively Italian-sounding names, like *bourdhétto* (fish sauced with tomato spiked with cayenne), *sofríto* (veal simmered with parsley, garlic and vinegar) and *pastitsádha* (a rich concoction of veal or cockerel stewed with onion and garlic, wine, tomato and cinnamon and served with thick macaroni), along with English puddings and *tsitsibýra* (ginger beer), served in some Listón cafés to go with a cricket game on the Spianádha.

In the old days, *bourdhétto*, *pastitsádha* and *sofríto* were party dishes prepared for a name day or special occasion by town folk. The country people were alarmingly poor and subsisted on a diet of wild greens, olive oil and bread, with an occasional rabbit or partridge. Even the more affluent ate far more sparingly than we do today. Surprisingly, many still hanker for 'poor people's food' – look for *tsigarélli* (sautéed greens with a touch of paprika).

The Corfiots prefer fruit for dessert and eat their sweets after the afternoon siesta or, at the risk of ruining their appetite, before dinner. These could be oriental pastries or ice cream, but the island is famous for its aromatic wild strawberries in late spring, *sykomaïdha* (fig bread) laced with grape must, brandy, ouzo and orange peel in autumn, and kumquats, fresh, glacéed or made into a bright orange liqueur that is unexpectedly delicious when added to fruit salads.

Diana Farr Louis and June Marinos are the authors of *Prospero's Kitchen: Mediterranean Cookery of the Ionian Islands from Corfu to Kythera.*

Restaurants

Eating out on Corfu can be hit or miss. All the restaurants have been personally, repeatedly and happily tested by Insight authors. The price guide is as follows: € = inexpensive; €€ = moderate; and €€€ = expensive.

Ághios Ioánnis

Spyros and Vasilis: Cuisine Française
Tel: 26610 52552/52438
On a hill in peaceful, rolling fields, near Tríklino and adjacent to Aqualand, is a surprise find: a fine French-with-a-Hellenic-twist restaurant. Start with pan-sautéed frogs' legs or mussels in cream. Follow that with the *Filet Spyros*, and finish with a *Soufflé au Grand Marnier*, a cheese platter or *Crêpes Suzettes* (if you want soufflés and crêpes, say so when you reserve a table). Extensive wine list. Open all year; veranda tables in summer. €€

Ághios Matthéos

Alonaki Bay Taverna
Tel: 26610 76118/9/75872
One of the locals' best-kept secrets until now, this little taverna, run by the Varagoulis family, shelters under windswept and stunted

trees above little Alonáki Bay. It serves up fresh fish, eels, octopus and tiny Lake Korissíon shrimp, and you'll never want to leave, but there are rooms to rent here. €

Agní
Toula
Tel: 26630 91350
Famous for its professional demeanour, nice line in hot *mezédhes* and the house special *garídhes* (shrimps) Toula – grilled prawns with spicy mixed-rice pilaf. Excellent bulk white wine and house desserts to round it off; open for lunch and supper much of the year. €€

Ághios Stéfanos Sinión
Eucalyptus (Evkalyptos)
North end of bay
Tel: 26630 82007
Housed in an old stone building, but with outdoor tables, weather permitting, this is probably the best, and best-value taverna in what can be a pretentious resort. They present a good mix of grilled seafood or meat, and Corfiot casserole dishes with innovative flavourings. Open May–Oct; best at lunch, as they tend to run out of food fairly early in the evening by Greek standards. €€

Avláki Bay
Cavo Barbaro (Fotis)
Tel: 26630 81905
An unusually good beach taverna, easy of access while touring the north coast, with welcoming service. A few pre-cooked dishes at lunch, like 'risotto' and *soudzoukákia*, more grills after dark, plus homemade *glyká koutalioú* (candied fruit). Seating on the lawn, and plenty of parking. The only thing 'barbarous' here can be the wind, as there's no shelter; check direction and strength before heading downhill. €

Boúkari
Spiros Karidis Fish Taverna
Tel: 26620 51205/51876
Since 1971 this has been 'the' place on the east coast for grilled fish, lobster, 'Corfiot sushi', and all else edible from the sea. Spiros, his son, Nektarios, and son-in-law, Christos, are beloved of a host of summer 'regulars' from northern Europe. €€

Gastoúri
Bella Vista
Tel: 26610 56232
Hilltop restaurant that lives up to its name, taking in a view extending from the Achilleion Palace to Epirus across the straits. Best for *mayireftá* meat dishes and grills, and a good choice if you've just visited the palace. Open Easter–Oct Tues–Sun; weekends only off-season. €€

Káto Korakiána
Etrusco
Tel: 26610 93342
Top-calibre nouvelle Italian cooking purveyed by the Bottrini family – Hector is the Gold Hat-winning master chef – served since 1992 at a carefully restored country manor. Specialities such as home-made cured meat, *timpano parpadellas* (pasta with duck and truffles) and a 200-label wine list don't come cheaply though – budget for a minimum of €30 each not including drinks. Open Apr–Oct, supper only; reservations essential. €€€

Kérkyra Town
Aegli Restaurant
23 Kapodhistríou Street
Tel: 26610 31949
Promoted as the oldest traditional restaurant in Kérkyra Town – it was established in 1812 – the Aegli is linen-napkin respectable and open all day. From the Corfiot specialities, try the veal or cockerel *pastitsáda*, veal *sofríto*, or *kléftiko* (lamb and onion fricassee). €€

Left: a meeting of like minds
Right: service at the Rex

Del Sole Ristorante
17 Guílford Street, Pórta Remoúnda
Tel: 26610 32411
The Corfiot Metallinou family owns and operates this superb Italian restaurant, specialising in homemade fresh pastas. Try penne with tomato sauce and basil, spaghetti pesto, macaroni with gorgonzola, the roca and Parmesan salad, prosciutto croquettes – and leave room for the house cheesecake or *panna cotta*. Supper all year, lunch also May–Oct. €€

En Plo
Ta Bánia tou Alékou/Faliráki Complex
Tel: 26610 8183
This is a most romantic café, with views of the Old Fortress and Vídhos islet, good snack-fare and, on weekends, live music. Open year round, 10am–2pm. €

Hryssomallis (alias **Babis**)
6 Nikifórou Theotókou
Tel: 26610 30342
The sign says a *zythopsitopolío* ('beer-hall–grill'), but it's also one of the last surviving traditional oven-food places in the old town: stews, *hórta*, *moussakás*, lamb offal, and so forth, all washed down with smooth but potent red wine. From the outside tables on the pedestrian street you can just see the Listón, while Venetian housefronts tower overhead; a typical bill won't run to more than €10–13 each. It's been around since 1839, and in the Statiris family since the 1950s; the Durrells ate here regularly during their 1930s stay on Corfu. €

Il Giardino
4 Vraïla Street
Tel: 26610 30723
Just uphill from the Archaeological Museum of Corfu, this predominantly locals-only Italian bistro seats diners in a quiet walled garden. The diverse menu also features some 10 variations on fillet steak. Open evenings only. €€

La Cucina
15 Guílford Street, Pórta Remoúnda
Tel: 26610 45029
Another great Italian bistro on Guílford Street. ...ain, homemade pasta is the star, and there ...some spectacular combinations on the menu: linguine with butterfly prawns, rocket, parsley, spring onions and a creamy *wasabi* sauce, or a pan-seared filet, and tortelloni with prosciutto. Feb–Nov, supper only. €€

La Famiglia
30 Maniarízi keh Arlióti Street (Kandoúni Bízi)
Tel: 26610 30270
Mr and Mrs Sandro and Maryo Campogiani run the town's most-popular mini-bistro, where pasta dishes featuring mature and baby clams *(vongole)*, an array of Italian antipasti and fresh quiches – plus puddings to die for – make reservations a must. (For return visitors, note: the restaurant has relocated two doors downhill.) €€

Mouragia
15 Arseníou Street, Mourághia District
Tel: 26610 33815
A good mix of seafood (with fresh and frozen items clearly indicated) and Corfiot *mayireftá* such as *sofríto* and *pastitsádha* at this all-year *ouzerí* popular with families and students. Inexpensive for any island, let alone Corfu's old town, and great sea views in the bargain. €

O Yiannis
43 Aghíon Iásonos and Sosipatroú Street, Anemómylos Quarter
Tel: 26610 31066
Open since the late 1970s, this is a grand old taverna where you troop off to the kitchen to view the contents of some 15–20 cooking pots. The veal (either in lemon or oregano sauce), *stifádo* (stew), and *gávros* (anchovies, in tomato and onion) are all good choices. €€

Rex Restaurant
66 Kapodhistríou Street
Tel: 26610 39649
Since 1932, the Rex has been serving Corfiot specialities with flair. Try their *arní stámnas* (lamb simmered in a ceramic crock), or fish *bourdhétto*. End with a baked apple or *ravaní*, a Greek cake drenched in syrup. The service is impeccable all day long. €€

The Five Sisters/Pénde Aderfés
151 Xen Stratigou Street
Tel: 26610 38263

Situated just off the port, this taverna caters mainly for locals and is run by the five Avgerinou sisters – Spyridoula, Eleftheria, Chryssoula, Sophia and Georgia. It is usually packed with diners tucking into enormous portions of charcoal-grilled lamb, beef, chicken, pork and sausage. Order a Greek salad, fries and wine from the barrel to go with the meat. €

Venetian Well
Platía Kremastí, northwest of the cathedral, Campiello district
Tel: 26610 44761
Tucked away through an arch, with outdoor tables around the namesake well, is arguably the town's most innovative – and expensive – cooking, generic Aegean with *nouvelle-cuisine* twists. The interior, following a 2001 overhaul, eclectically draws on several oriental traditions. Recipes change yearly, depending on the proprietor's winter travels and inspiration, but in past seasons have encompassed duck breast with dried fruit, whole-grain rice *dolmádhes*, or pork chop with sun-dried tomatoes and peppers. An expensive wine list pushes this into the splurge category, but with the enchanted setting, there's no better place in town to fall in love with Corfu – or your dining companion. Mar–Oct, supper only. €€€

Kontókali
Roula
Tel: 26610 91832
On the beach, overlooking Gouvia Marina, this is one of the island's best fish tavernas, with a daily catch, lobster, grilled octopus and marinated anchovies, all fresh. Open year round; reservations advised. €€

Lefkími
Maria
Riverbank, south quay
Tel: 26620 22150
Ideal for an inexpensive but tasty lunch of *mayireftá* (baked pork chops, baked fish, green beans, good bulk wine) while touring the far south; tables are under the trees overlooking the river. Maria herself, a traditionally dressed granny, is a never-ending fount of risqué anecdotes, and a crash course in

baroquely elaborate Greek swearing comes free with your meal. €

Nissáki
Mitsos
Tel: 26630 91240
On the little rock-outcrop 'islet' *(nissáki)*, this ordinary-looking beachside taverna stands out for cheerful service from two partners. There's a high turnover which ensures that the fare, which includes fried local fish and well-executed *sofríto*, is always fresh. Open Apr–Oct, lunch and dinner . €

Paleá Períthia
Foros
Just off the central plaza
Tel: 26630 98373
This all-but-abandoned, perfectly preserved stone village on the north slopes of Mt Pandokrátor has two tavernas. This is

the more down-to-earth, a little taverna-*ouzerí* specialising in its own cheese, one cooked dish per day, a few *píttas* (turnovers) and a choice of grills. The food's perhaps not the best in the interior, but it's a supremely atmospheric setting with civil service. €

Paxí
Erimitis Sunset View Bar
Lákka-Gaïos Road
Tel: 69777 53499
Located about 1km (½ mile) off the main road and right on top of the cliffs, this restaurant has an unbelievable sunset veiw. Open 11am till very late in season, a full food menu is offered after 4pm. €

Right: three members of The Five Sisters taverna

Kafeneío Bournaós
Magazi
Tel: 26620 31906
It's well worth driving up to the tiny hamlet of Magazi to enjoy a Greek coffee and a traditional 'spoon sweet' *(glykó tou koutalioú)* at this quaint, 1950s-vintage Greek *kafeneíon*. €€

Kafezacaroplasteion To Briki
Gaïos
Tel: 26620 32255
Serving coffee, *soumádha* (a cool, almond drink), fresh yoghurt, rice pudding and a cake called *Boltsevíkos* since 1962, this is a delightful family-run patisserie. €

La Boca
Lákka Bay
Tel: 26620 31991
Chef Valter De Cian hails from Turin but worked nine years in Paris, and the French influence is reflected in his eclectic menu. The view of Lákka Bay and the wine cellar here are also impressive. €€

Mambo
Gaïos
Tel: 26620 32670
Lovely waiting staff, excellent Greek specialities, and a seat right on Gaïos's old harbour for lunch or dinner make this a great place to dine and people watch. €

Taka-Taka
Gaïos
Tel: 26620 32329

Kostas Vlachopoulos's speciality is spit-roasted meats, from lamb to chicken to suckling pig. The bar is festive here, and the garden leafy and cool. €€

Vassilis
Longós quay
Tel: 26620 31587
Now often known as Kostakis after the son who's taken it over, this has grown from a grilled fish specialist to an all-round taverna with imaginative recipes including stuffed mushrooms and peppers, baked meat dishes and various pies. Often hosts excellent live music at Sunday lunch, and always has proper table linen (a rarity in Greece). €€

Strinýlas
Elm Tree Taverna (Iy Ftelia)
Tel: 26630 71454
The Koskinas family open all year here, and the menu features grilled meats from the Épirot province of Ioánnina. *Sofríto* and wild boar *stifádo* are specialities. And be sure to order a white or red house barrel wine (have a designated driver, though – the road downhill from Mt Pandokrátor is a winding one). Open all year (weekends only in winter). €€

Atmospheric Bistros
In Kérkyra there are four venues for drinks, light meals and snacks that provide much in terms of atmosphere and ambience. Small, al fresco bistros, these are all lovely romantic places for couples to go for the evening and linger into the night.

The sober and sensible residents of Corfu, of course, are largely dependent upon the summer tourist trade to support them year round, and have found themselves finan‑ cially strapped in recent seasons due to the decline in 'quality' (read 'high-spending') tourism on the island. Consequently, they are not inclined to spend their hard-earned wages on €6 cocktails and the steep cover charges that prevail at the *bouzoúkia*, or *kéndra*, the live Greek music nightclubs. Nor will any but the very young find the dance club area particularly appealing.

The club scene in Kérkyra is all but quarantined to the string of DJ-and-dance establishments that line Ethnikís Antistásseos Street in the New Port – forming the so-called 'straight' district – and even these venues, except at the height of summer, are to be found humming only very late on Friday and Saturday nights. Turn up at Corfu's two or three bouzouki clubs before midnight, even at weekends, and you will be greeted by cavernous, silent, dark nightclub space. 'Come back around 2am,' say the waiters. And at a couple of places it is worth doing so: at **Notes Live** or **Ekati**, the two truly Greek venues on Corfu, where you will be treated to authentic, contemporary Greek club music, albeit for a considerable price.

There is a much greater selection of local nightlife of a more sedentary variety on the island. The Corfiots themselves generally prefer to relax out of doors in the evening, sitting at one of the bars and cafés on the Spianádha in Kérkyra, or by the sea all over the island. They sip tall drinks and nibble on *mezédhes* (little appetisers) into the wee hours, talking with friends and family and listening to recorded music.

The following annotated list of nighttime venues does not aspire to be inclusive. Corfu comprises a large and bustling constellation of resorts, hotels and night-spots in summer – and the sampling below is just a fraction of what's on offer. It represents the pick of the best that the island has to offer, and consists of a reliable selection of venues that are well established, not the 'here this year, gone next' variety, nor the 'here next year, but under new management' kind of place.

The **Art Café and Bar** (tel: 26610 49366), is in the garden adjacent to the Municipal Gallery. €€

The **Old Fortress Café** (tel: 26610 48550) is near the Church of St George, inside the Old Fortress proper, but open till the wee hours. €€

En Plo (tel: 26610 81813) is on the sea below the Palace of St Michael and St George and the Art Café and Bar garden. €€

The **Nautilus** (tel: 26610 49707) is in the Anemómylos Quarter, on the sea at the southern tip of Garítsa Bay. €€

NIGHTLIFE

For visitors who are accustomed to the all-summer-long, seven-nights-a-week club scene of the Cycladic islands, the largest Dodecanese and, certainly, entire sections of Athens and Greece's other larger mainland towns and cities, Corfiot nights may seem quite tame by comparison in all but a few isolated areas – and then the tawdry, beer-soaked festivities of, say, Kávos, may just put you off your night out on the town.

Left: local wine. **Above:** street sweets: *loukoumádes* for sale on the roadside

Kanóni

Casino at the Corfu Holiday Palace Hotel
Corfu Holiday Palace Hotel
Tel: 26610 46941/2
Originally opened in 1961 in the Ahíllion, the casino has long since moved to its present location in Kanóni. It was privately operated until 1983, but is now an EOT (National Tourist Board of Greece) holding, offering American and French roulette, blackjack, poker and 50 slot machines. Open daily: slot machines noon–3am; other games 8.30pm–3am.

Kassiópi

Kostas' Music Bar
Main port road
Tel: 26630 81955
This is a deafeningly loud, initially ordinary-looking little bar that is generally packed with British tourists of a certain age. But there is a surprise in store if you venture inside – owner Kostas, or 'Bakkas', Saranginos dances the *zeybékiko* (the 'dance of the drunken man') like a Levantine Nureyev. Alexis Zorbas lives!

Kérkyra

Alkis Billiards and Accessories
14 Kapodhistríou Street
Tel: 26610 33883
Located right on the Spianádha, this is the place to go for billiards, with drinks. A little rough-and-ready in terms of clientele – but it's air conditioned!

Aperito
14 Ethnikís Antistásseos Street
New Port
Tel: 26610 40487
Ioannis Ionas's popular bar catering for the teens to thirties crowd, serves cold drinks, cocktails and coffees – and you can hear yourself think here. Open Mon–Fri 9pm–3.30am; later on Sat and Sun.

Au Bar/Bora Bora
34 Ethnikís Antistasséos Street
New Port
Tel: 26610 80909
Open from midnight on, this low-ceilinged, wood-and-stone dance club's been going strong for 25 years. A drinks-and-music only venue, the outdoor bar attracts a slightly more mature crowd. Often hosts foreign DJs in high season. Open daily Apr–Oct, weekend only otherwise.

Boem
28 Kapodhistríou Street
Tel: 26610 46226
E-mail: cafe_online@yahoo.com
This chic bar-cum-internet café (with other locations in Moraïtika and Kassiópi) is a gathering place for Corfu's computer-literate of all nationalities. This place is made what it is by owners Kostas and Spyros's friendly multilingual hospitality (and Eleni's coffee). Open 10am–1am in high season.

Café Grec
5 Kapodhistríou Street
Tel: 26610 36645
Located just behind the Listón, and open all day (until 1am) for Portioli coffees, drinks and, eventually, cocktails, this is a well-loved little see-and-be-seen venue.

Cavalieri Hotel Roof Garden
Cavalieri Hotel

Above: ready for an evening out

4 Kapodhistríou Street
Tel: 26610 39041/39336

One of the most romantic (and comprehensive) vantage points in the city, this roof garden overlooks the Spianádha, the Old Fortress and Garítsa Bay. The Cavalieri serves light meals, ice-cream, drinks and cocktails – with a lovely view. Open May–Oct, 6.30pm–4am.

Cristal

52 Ethnikís Antistásseos Street
New Port
Tel: 26610 43150

A huge, well-established disco-with-swimming-pool, the Hippodrome opens at midnight, but really doesn't start cooking till hours later. The musical format progresses from ambient to House. In the winter months, its clientele is made up mostly of Corfiot teenagers, while in summer, it becomes the popular wee-hours haunt of Italian and English visitors.

Ekati

Alykés Potamoú Street
Tel: 26610 45920

This upmarket, modern Greek-style nightclub on the outskirts of Kérkyra features excellent live *bouzoúki* bands with vocalists, and caters for a very well-heeled, over-30 Greek crowd. Cocktails and bottles of whisky, dinners and snacks are all expensive. It's really only worth going very late at weekends (around 1–5am) and in winter it's only open on Friday and Saturday anyway. It's also a good idea to phone ahead for reservations.

Hook

5 Kapodhistríou Street
Tel: 26610 47131

An elegant little bar that spills out into the Spianádha, next door to the Cavalieri Hotel, the Hook features rock music, a full bar and Carlsberg on tap. Also open in the morning for coffee.

Magnet

102 Kapodhistríou Street
Tel: 26610 45295

At the noisy (duelling rock music at adjacent bars) end of the Listón is Magnet, a popular if pricy café/bar that's packed soon after the sun goes down. Order drinks and cocktails here after dinner and before moving on to the 'Straight's' dance club district.

Netoikos Internet Café

14 Kaloherétou Street
(opposite St Spyridon's)
Tel: 26610 47479

At €3 per DSL hour, internet access is reasonable and speedy here; and the rates are also low for printing and scanning. The café also features a hip full-service bar, where young Corfiots mingle, Mon–Sat 10am–midnight, Sun 6pm–midnight.

Privilege

42 Ethnikís Antistasséos Street
New Port
Tel: 26610 80780/1

This club, which opened in the late 1990s, has been designed to have the appearance of an archaeological site on the Nile – wild! It attracts a slightly more mature, slightly trendier crowd than many of the neighbouring venues. Next door, the management has opened Smooth, a convenient restaurant-cum-snack-bar for those who want a nice bite to eat before or after dancing and drinking. Open midnight until the wee hours, and busy at weekends; more Greek than foreign sounds.

Tzávros
Notes Live

Paleokastrítsa Highway
(just north of Gouviá)
Tel: 26610 91733

Like the Ekati, Corfu By Night is an authentic Greek *skyládhiko* or roadhouse – that is to say it is devoted to heavily amplified *bouzoúki* ensembles and Greek vocalists; sometimes there are Greek dancers as well. It is in full swing only on Friday night and weekends from around 12.30–4am. This is the perfect place to see Corfiots enjoying their preferred genre of music. You should arrange for a taxi to pick you up after the show, and call in advance for programme information and reservations. Drinks, by the glass or full bottles, and food are pricy and there is also a cover charge.

CALENDAR OF EVENTS

The Greek year is delightfully interspersed with ancient, Christian or patriotic holidays: Greek Orthodox Easter, the anniversary of a popular revolution or local victory, or the name day of a beloved saint. These name days, or saints' days – *yiortés* in Greek – are very important to Greeks, who barely note their own birthdays but entertain family and friends lavishly on the evening of their own saint's name day. Often, entire villages turn out – with parades, a street fair, and church services – to honour a saint whose church is pre-eminent in their town.

Four great annual processions are held to honour St Spýridhon *(see page 16)*, and his name day, 12 December, is all but a pan-island holiday, since so many Corfiots bear the name Spiridon, Spiros or Spiridoula.

January

1 Ághios Vasílios (St Basil). Holiday gifts are exchanged and the *vassilópitta* – a cake with a coin baked in it for luck – is ritually cut.
6 Ta Fóta (Epiphany). National holiday. Blessing of the waters, to commemorate Christ's baptism, at the little port of Mandhráki, beneath the Old Fortress in Corfu/Kérkyra Town.

February

2 Ypapandí (Candlemas). The Presentation of Christ at the Temple. Festivities at the Church of Ypapandí in Kommémo.

Variable date. Apókries. The three-week period preceding Greek Orthodox Lent is Greece's Carnival Season. Fancy dress parties, masked balls, parades with floats and marching bands, and peculiarly Corfiot variations on the Carnival theme.

March

8 Aghía Theodhóra (St Theodora). The saint's relics are carried around Kérkyra.
25 Greek Independence Day; also **Evangelismós (Annunciation)**. National holiday commemorating the beginning of the Greek Revolution against the Ottoman Turks in 1821.
Variable date: Katharí Dheftéra (Clean Monday). National holiday marking the first day of Lenten fasting, seven weeks before Easter. Kite-flying and picnics with special Lenten fare. Carnival parade at Perouládhes.

April

Variable date. Greek Orthodox Easter. Almost always in April.
Palm Sunday. Procession with St Spýridhon's relics *(see page 16)* and marching bands through Kérkyra; feast of salt cod.
Megáli Evdomádha (Holy Week). Many Greeks fast for this entire week, especially on Good Friday, which resembles a day of national mourning throughout the country.
Holy Tuesday. Choir recitals at the church of Ágios Spyrídonos, the Church of Agía Paraskeví and the Metropolitan Cathedral.
Holy Wednesday. Concert of hymns by the Municipal Choir at the Municipal Theatre.
Holy Thursday. Service of the Twelve Gospels is held at the Catholic Cathedral, in Platía Dhimarhíou.
Megáli Paraskeví (Good Friday). National holiday. Sombre rites surrounding the *Epitáfios* (Christ's Funeral Bier). Biers from many churches, accompanied by marching bands, process through Kérkyra.
Megálo Sávvato (Holy Saturday). Procession of St Spýridhon's relics through Kérkyra *(see page 16)*; various services and traditional events. At midnight the Lenten fast is broken with red-dyed eggs, special lamb tripe soup and loaves baked in the shape of doves. Festivities, complete with fireworks and marching bands, are best viewed from the Spianádha.
Páskha (Greek Orthodox Easter). National holiday. The most important day of the Greek

Left: parading in Corfiot costume

year is celebrated with feasting and joyful recreation. Corfiot churches process icons of the Resurrection.

Easter Monday. Processions with noisy and dangerous fireworks.

Easter Tuesday. At 5pm, St Spýridhon's relics are returned to the Church of Ághios Spyrídhonos.

Friday after Easter. *Zoödhóhos Pighí* (The Font of Life) celebration at Paleokastrítsa.

Sunday after Easter. St Thomas. Procession and festivities at Epískepsi and Sidhári.

May

1 May Day/Labour Day. National holiday. Workers' parades and trips to the countryside to gather flowers and foliage for May wreaths.

21 SS Constantine and Helen. This saints' day also celebrates the union of the Ionian Islands with Greece.

June

Variable date: Pendekostí (Pentecost/Whit Sunday). Celebrated seven weeks after Easter with festivities throughout Corfu.

Aghíou Pnévmatos (Whit Monday). National holiday.

12 Ághios Onoúfrios. Festivities at Pélekas.

29 SS Peter and Paul. Festivities at many villages throughout Corfu; major festival at Gaïos, Paxí.

Variable dates June into July: Divertimenti on Corfu (tel: 26610 90820; www.chamber musicholidays.com).

July

2 Panaghía Vlahernón. Festivities at Aharávi, Garítsa and Kamára, and Fondána on Paxí.

12 St Spýridhon. One of several days dedicated annually to the island's patron saint *(see page 16)*.

13 Aghía Marína. Festivities at Avliótes, Benítses, Sparterá and Kérkyra.

August

1–6 Christ The Saviour. Six days of festivities at the Monastery of the Pandokrátor.

6 Metamórfosi (Transfiguration of Christ). Festivities in the Campiello Quarter of Kérkyra and throughout Corfu.

10 Varkarola. Concert of *kandádhes*, traditional Ionian Island songs, from watercraft anchored in Garítsa Bay.

11 St Spýridhon. Yet another of the days dedicated to the memory of the saint. Procession in Corfu/Kérkyra Town; festivities throughout the island.

15 The Dormition/Assumption of The Virgin Mary. National holiday with festivities the length and breadth of Corfu.

September

In September, the International Festival of Classical Music is held on Paxí.

Variable dates in early September: Divertimenti on Corfu.

October

28 'Ohi' ('No') Day. National holiday commemorating Metaxas' standing up to Mussolini and the Italian invasion (with his famous 'No!') in 1940.

November

15 Start of the Fast of the Nativity ('Little Lent').

17 Polytechnion Day. School holiday and early business closings. Commemorates the sit-in and subsequent massacre at the Athens Polytechnical School which led to the fall of the 1970s junta.

December

6 Ágios Nikólaos (St Nicholas). Christmas festivities the length and breadth of Corfu.

12 St Spýridhon's Day. Local holiday. Two-day festivities in Kérkyra. Festivities in Kavvadádes, Spartýlas, Kanáli, Vasilátika and Velonádes.

25 Hristoúgema (Christmas).

26 Gathering of the Virgin's Entourage.

31 New Year's Eve.

Above Right: lighting a candle at Ághios Spýridhonos

Practical
Information

GETTING THERE

Unfortunately, there are currently no scheduled airline flights from New York or England (apart from internal flights from Athens and Thessaloníki) to Corfu, but in the brave new world of no-frills carriers, and with over 10,000 foreign residents on this island, this could very well change, with rumours abounding of easyJet inaugurating links with England in coming years. For the moment, most British travellers take charter flights, which link a dozen British airports to Corfu (around 3 hours' flight time). The only regularly scheduled flights to Corfu on commercial carriers depart from Athens (45 minutes). If you are travelling from North America, you might find it just as cheap to fly to London and pick up a charter flight from there. Aegan Airlines have a few direct connections to Corfu from northern Italy, which may be convenient for North American travellers connecting through Milan. With careful planning and an eye to layover times, it's usually not necessary to spend a night in Athens en route unless you explicitly wish to.

Especially coming from North America, you will find that fares drop considerably if your flight includes a one-stop itinerary via Rome, Frankfurt or Zurich (these are the most common hubs). Additionally, recourse to reliable internet travel sites such as www. expedia.com/co.uk, www.travelselect.com, www. cheapflights.co.uk or www.a2b.com should turn up a number of attractive options. Or try the airlines' own sites; most offer a slight discount for booking on line.

Most airports in Germany and Britain, as well as the Netherlands, Italy, Scandanavia, Switzerland, the Czech Republic and even Russia or Poland offer something weekly or more frequently between Easter and mid-October. It is almost always cheaper to use a direct charter package to the island than a scheduled fare, even if you don't use the basic accommodation included.

By Air from Greece

The Greek domestic carrier Aegean Airlines flies several times daily from Athens and (far less often) Thessaloníki to Corfu. Aegean Airlines provides two user-friendly daily departures from Athens throughout the year. Flight time from Athens is just under an hour, and prices are fairly steep (typically €160 return in summer) for the distance involved, though you can occasionally find promotional fares of €130 or even €100. With the recent decrease in flight frequency, it is necessary to book at least two weeks in advance, even during spring or autumn.

Useful phone numbers and websites:

Ioannis Kapodistrias Airport, Corfu, general info, tel: 26610 30180

Aegean Airlines, airport, tel: 26610 27100

Olympic Airways, Polylá 11, Kérkyra, tel: 26610 38694

Olympic Airways, airport, tel: 26610 37398

Olympic Airways, nationwide reduced-rate number: 801 1144444

Aegean Airlines, nationwide reduced-rate number: 801 1120000

www.olympic-airways.gr

www.aegeanair.com

By Road

The nearest Greek mainland port of call for Corfu is Igoumenítsa, which is served by regularly scheduled bus service from Athens and Thessaloníki. There are also car ferry connections to Corfu from Pátra, which is much more quickly accessible from Athens by train, bus or private car (3–4 hours depending on traffic).

KTEL (Intercity Bus Service): for information in Athens, tel: 210 512-9443; in Igoumenítsa, tel: 26650 22309; in Ioánnina, tel: 0651 26404; in Pátras, tel: 2610 222271

By Sea

There's a wide variety of fairly consistent car ferry, catamaran and hydrofoil links between Corfu and Pátras, Igoumenítsa and (rarely)

Left: forward planning

Saghiáda on the Greek mainland, as well as with Ancona, Bari, Brindisi, Trieste and Venice in Italy. Domestic ferries connect Corfu also with the nearby Dhiapóndia islets to the north and Paxí to the south. The main destination on Corfu is Kérkyra's New Port, but Lefkími in the south is also useful, especially for car-drivers approaching from Igoumenítsa.

In season, there are frequent (almost two-hourly) car-ferry services from Igoumenítsa to Kérkyra; crews are (unusually for Greece) courteous and efficient, and fares for a car and driver together run at about €22. The journey takes 1 hour 45 minutes, though you can trim this – and the fare – to about an hour and €13 by using the crossing to Lefkími which operates about six times daily. Hydrofoils (no cars) between Igoumenítsa and Kérkyra take half the time at roughly double the price.

For getting to the Dhiapóndia islets, there is a slow car ferry from Kérkyra (2–4 times weekly depending on season), though most people visit on the passenger-only caiques out of Sidári or Ághios Stéfanos Avliotón (3–6 days weekly depending on demand).

The Paxí are served by at least five slow weekly ferries year-round from Kérkyra; in season this rises to at least two daily, with an extra hydrofoil departure thrown in. In season, the Igoumenítsa–Paxí sea lane is also served by both sorts of craft, which may involve triangular routings out of Lefkími or Kérkyra.

From Italy, at least one shipping company calls at Kérkyra's New Port every day except perhaps January and February. Fares vary widely depending on speed and comfort of craft and, of course, according to start-point (Bari/Brindisi are the shortest and cheapest,

Venice/Trieste the most expensive). Most, though not all, departures are overnight; budget a minimum of €120 for two people in a cabin plus a small car, taxes included.

International ferry schedules tend to be quite reliable, though the most current information source are the various companies' websites. Printed domestic schedules (rarely) seen in Greece tend to be obsolete or fantastic (in the literal sense) the minute they're off the press; the only firm information on sailings is to be had by strolling down to the quayside ticket booths in person, or by contacting the following *limenarhía* or port authorities:

Kérkyra: tel: 26610 32655/30096/30481
Lefkími: tel: 26620 23277
Igoumenítsa: tel: 26650 99400
Pátras: tel: 2610 341002 or 341024
Paxí (Gaïos): tel: 26620 32259
Saghiádha (July–Aug): tel: 26640 51217

TRAVEL ESSENTIALS

When to Visit

Corfu is at its best in spring, from Greek Orthodox Easter to June, when the island is awash with flowers, and then again after the high season, in September and October. Online, check the weather forecast at www.noa.gr.

Visas and Passports

European Union, Australian, New Zealand, Canadian, US and most other non-European Union visitors need only a valid passport to visit Corfu; non-EU visitors are stamped in and out upon arrival/departure, which affords them an informal, 90-day tourist 'visa'.

Customs

Duty-free restrictions no longer apply within the EU, though goods carried must be for personal use only (officials have their own guidelines for what may reasonably be considered for personal use), and spot checks for illegal drugs may still occur. Entering Greece from outside the EU you are allowed to bring with you, duty-free: 200 cigarettes or 50 cigars; 1 litre (35fl oz) of spirits or 2 litres (70fl oz) of wine; 50g (1¾ fl oz) of perfume; 250ml (8¾fl oz) of eau de cologne; one camera and film; one pair of binoculars; a portable musical instrument; a portable radio or tape recorder;

	Average Temperature (°C/°F)	Average Rainy Days
January	12/53	12
February	15/59	12
March	13/57	9
April	16/60	9
May	19/66	6
June	23/73	4
July	26/79	1
August	26/79	1
September	23/73	5
October	19/66	11
November	15/59	11
December	12/54	15

a laptop; sports equipment, and, with a veterinarian's certificate, dogs and cats. When carrying medicines, be sure to bring along the corresponding physicians' prescriptions; non-prescription medicines containing codeine are not permitted. You may import an unlimited amount of foreign currency, but if you intend to leave with foreign currency units amounting to over US$1,000, you must declare this amount upon entering Greece. It is a severely punishable offence to remove antiquities of any size or value from Greece.

Clothing

The Corfiot summer lasts from June to September, though light rain falls at both ends of the season, and a showerproof coat comes in handy. In high season it can be very hot, humid and sticky, so the most comfortable clothing is lightweight and made of natural fabrics – and be sure to bring enough, because laundry and dry-cleaning services, except at the top hotels, are primitive and slow. Pack sturdy shoes with crêpe soles for walking, or hiking boots if you plan more strenuous treks; sandals and plastic water shoes for the beach (to protect against sea urchins); high-SFP sunblock; a sunhat; extra pairs of prescription spectacles; snorkelling gear and a beach towel if you want; and modest clothing for visiting churches and monasteries – at least one long-sleeved garment for both men and women, plus long trousers and an over-the-knee skirt/dress, according to gender.

GETTING ACQUAINTED

Geography

Kérkyra lies 39º 38' North and 19º 54' East. The island has an area of about 593sq km (230sq miles), with a population of around 115,000, of whom some 33,000 live in the capital (2001 census) and of which a staggering 10 percent are foreign-born. The prefecture of Corfu, Paxí, Andípaxi, Othoní, Eríkoussa and Mathráki constitutes the third most densely populated prefecture in Greece.

Religion

Unlike the rest of Greece, which is almost solely Greek Orthodox, Corfu has a significant Roman Catholic population, mostly of Mal-

tese origin, who have their own cathedral in the capital. There are also Anglican, Evangelical and Jewish communities and congregations, all with their own places of worship.

How Not To Offend

The Ionian islands are more conservative than many of the Greek islands further south. Very modest dress is required in order to enter most monasteries and churches on the island; toplessness is tolerated on some beaches but is not the general rule; and there is only one openly nudist beach in all of Corfu *(see Itinerary 11, Page 52)*. There is also a visible police presence throughout the island, and drunkenness and other public misbehaviour is not tolerated (except, arguably, in Kávos).

How to Stay Safe

The British Consul on Corfu hands out a travel advisory leaflet for visitors featuring a checklist for a safe visit: 1) Bring sufficient funds. 2) When hiring a vehicle, boat or moped, check it's road- or sea-worthy, has sufficient insurance, and comes with safety equipment. 3) Women should not walk home alone at night, nor accept lifts from strangers or casual acquaintances. 4) When visiting historic sites, remember that these are the favoured haunts of bag-snatchers and thieves. 5) Do not get involved with drugs in Greece. 6) Do not

Above: in the Campiello district

expect to find work easily. 7) Respect Greece's customs regulations. 8) Respect Greece's laws in general. 9) Too much sun mixed with alcohol usually results in serious health problems.

Money Matters
Currency
The currency of Greece is the euro (*evró* in Greek), subdivided into 100 cents *(leptá)*. Euros come as notes of 500, 200, 100, 50, 20, 10 and 5, while coins come as 2 euros, 1 euro, and 50, 20, 10, 5, 2 and 1 cent(s).

Credit Cards
Many credit cards – VISA preferred – are accepted at upmarket hotels, restaurants (but not *tavernes*) and shops, but cash is always preferred on Corfu, and will often earn you a discount on goods. Note: always carry some small-denomination notes as taxi drivers will not change anything above a 50-euro note.

Cash Machines
Almost all Corfiot bank branches – and there are many – have ATMs, though they may not always be in working order.

Tipping
Leaving a tip of 10–15 percent of the bill is customary for sterling service.

GETTING AROUND

Taxis
Corfu has a well organised and reliable radio taxi service, vastly superior to the one in Athens. Drivers are apt to be more honest than their Athenian counterparts, and lost or forgotten property may actually be returned. The Association of Corfu Radiotaxi Owners issues a pamphlet which lists fares to and from various destinations, as these rates on Corfu are set, not measured by meter. Ask for this pamphlet if you plan to make frequent use of radio taxis. Within Kérkyra town the standard urban rates – posted on a laminated dashboard placard – apply. There are taxi ranks at the new and old ports, at the south end of the Spianáda and on Platía San Rocco.

Radio Taxi, 24-hour service, tel: 26610 33811–2

Taxi Ranks
Corfu town, tel: 26610 33811–2
Northern Corfu, tel: 26630 32400
Southern Corfu, tel: 26610 75210

Bus
There are two fleets of buses on Corfu: blue urban buses, with a terminus in San Rocco Square (tel: 26610 39859), which serve Kérkyra and its suburbs; and green-and-cream long-distance buses, with a terminus on Avramíou Street (tel: 26610 30627/39985/39862), which ply further afield and serve the rest of the island. A copy of the most recent bus schedule can be found in any issue of *The Corfiot*, an English-language monthly magazine that can be picked up from any newsagent in the capital. Tickets for blue buses are sold at kiosks on the square; for long-distance buses, they're sold on board.

Car
You may call or fax ahead, or book on an international website and have a hire car waiting for you at the airport on Corfu. You can arrange for one through your hotel but, in high season, cars may not be available unless booked in advance. It is worth paying the higher rate for all-inclusive insurance coverage.

Major international car-hire chains and a few local one-offs worth contacting include: **Avis**: New Port, tel: 26610 24404, fax: 26610 26826, airport: 26610 42007, www.avis.com
Budget: 32 Polyhroníou Konstandá, tel: 26610 28282, fax: 26610 28489, airport: 26610 28208, www.drivebudget.com
Eurodollar: Old Port, tel: 26610 46748
Europcar: 32 Venizélou, tel: 26610 46931, fax: 26610 46934, airport: 26610 46440, www.europcar.com
Hertz: Tripouléíka district, tel: 26610 38388, airport: 26610 35547, fax: 26610 24477, www.hertz.com
Luangia Rents: Dhassia, tel: 26610 93969/97530, www.luangia@luangia.gr
National/Alamo: 38 Venizélou, tel: 26610 49651, fax: 26610 49653, www.national car.com
InterEurope: tel: 26610 24000, airport: 26610 36689
Sunrise: New Port, tel: 26610 26511/26610 44325

Petrol and Parking: There are ample petrol stations throughout Corfu. Parking in the capital is an endurance test; the only uncontrolled spaces tend to be out near the British Cemetery – otherwise resign yourself to using the fee area on the Spianádha, or at the Old Port.

HOURS AND HOLIDAYS

Business Hours

Government agencies are open weekdays 8am–2pm; banks 8am–2.30pm Monday to Thursday and 8am–2pm Friday; shop hours (which can vary by half an hour seasonally) are from around 9am–2pm and 5.30–8.30pm Tuesday, Thursday and Friday, and from 8.30am–2.30pm Monday, Wednesday and Saturday; department stores and supermarkets are open 8am–8pm, Monday to Friday and from 8am–6pm on Saturday. Call individual places of interest and museums for their opening hours (as far as possible these have been included in the itineraries section of this guide). Kiosks open very early and close very late throughout the main tourist season.

Public Holidays

All banks, government offices, shops and most sites close for the following: New Year's Day, 1 January; Epiphany, 6 January; First Monday in Lent, moveable; Greek Independence Day, 25 March; Good Friday, moveable; Greek Orthodox Easter, moveable; Easter Monday, moveable; Labour Day, 1 May; Pentecost (Whit Monday), moveable; Feast of the Dormition of the Virgin, 15 August; 'Ohi' Day, 28 October; Christmas Day, 25 December; Gathering of the Virgin's Entourage, 26 December; and, unofficially, St Spýridhon's Days, 11 August and 12 December.

ACCOMMODATION

The best advice for first-time visitors is to stay in Kérkyra Town for the first part of your visit; then, after four or five days, relocate to a congenial beach resort or – taking things to remote extremes – to Paxí or even one of the Dhiapóndia islets. Like most of Greece, Corfu (except arguably for the town itself) offers great value for money accommodation-wise,

and you shouldn't dismiss a luxury hotel out of hand; a price that would get you no more than a grim closet in London or New York will net you a superb bungalow with a view or a characterful room near the Spianádha.

It's wise to book well in advance, either direct or through a travel agent *(see page 96)*. There are numerous rooms and apartments to rent on Corfu, but only local travel agents will know who is renting something attractive and reputable, year in year out. You can always take the lazy way out and book a cheap-and-cheerful, all-inclusive beach holiday through a package operator in Britain, but you will usually find yourself restricted to the north coast between Sidhári and Kassiópi, and the far south around Benítses, Messongí, Ághios Yeórghios Argyrádhes or (shudder) Kávos.

In the following lists, € = inexpensive, €€ = moderate, €€€ = expensive; unless otherwise indicated, establishments are only open April to October.

Aharávi

Acharávi Beach Hotel
Tel: 26630 63102/63124/63126
Fax: 26630 63461
www.greekislands.com
This 129-room, beach-front complex features two pools, a restaurant serving breakfast and dinner, and 23 apartments comprising two bedrooms and kitchenettes. All rooms have AC. €€

St George's Bay Country Club Hotel
PO Box 40
Tel: 26630 63203/63225
Fax: 26630 63540

Right: basic needs met here

This cloister-like arrangement of stone bungalows and villas, surrounded by extensive gardens, is right on the endless beach at Aharávi. It caters primarily for German visitors and has a pool, tennis and an excellent beachfront restaurant (Prospero's, tel: 26630 63247, ext. 16), open for all meals. €€€

Benitses
Ionian Hotel Costa Blu
Tel: 26610 72672
Fax: 26610 71223
www.holidays-corfu.com
The Costa Blu comprises 48 suites, immense verandahs, sea views towards the mainland, and every amenity. Located 12km (7 miles) south of Kérkyra Town, this 5-star complex currently offers very reasonable rates. €€

Dhafníla/Komméno
Hotel Nefeli
Tel: 26610 91033
Fax: 26610 90290
The pretty, salmon-pink Nefeli – 45 rooms housed in a lovely modern building – is located on the ritziest section of the east coast and shares some of the perks of nearby 4- and 5-star hotels: the Nefeli features balconies, spacious gardens, pool with a poolside bar, and great service: only some rooms with AC. €€

Dhassiá
Grecotel Dafnila Bay Thalasso
Tel: 26610 90321–4
Fax: 26610 91026
www.grecotel.gr
Part of the respected Grecotel chain, renovated in 1999, this 260-room-and-bungalow complex caters for families. 11km (7 miles) from the capital, it is luxurious and facilities include multiple restaurants and bars, child care, thalassotherapy spa, fitness activities and a private beach. Half board. €€€

Érmones
Sunmarotel Ermones
Tel: 26610 94241
Fax: 26610 94248
E-mail: ermones@otenet.gr
Another of the island's premier hotels, this 600-bed hotel and bungalow complex 17km (10½ miles) from the capital is set above Érmones Bay. A téléférique plies between the clifftop and the beach, serving the bungalows arranged in tiers. The hotel has two restaurants, a health and fitness centre, tennis courts, sauna and jacuzzi, air-conditioning and sea views. Half-board included. €€€

Glyfádha/Pélekas
Menigos Resort
Tel: 26610 95074/94083
Fax: 26610 94933
Open April through October, this 700-bed/ 141-bungalow complex sprawls through gardens along the entire length of beautiful Glyfádha Beach, some 20km (12 miles) from the capital. The self-catering bungalows, which are individually owned but let to visitors, are quickly snapped up, so you will need to fax Mr Koulouris well in advance to make your reservation. €€

Gouviá
Louis Corcyra Beach Hotel
Tel: 26610 90196
Fax: 26610 91591
www.louishotels.com
Not far from Gouviá's excellent marina and located right on the beach, this 260-room member of the Louis hotel chain is 13km (8 miles) north of the capital. The hotel, spread over two main buildings, has in-house restaurants and bars, full air-conditioning and gorgeous public rooms. Leisure facilities include pools, tennis and squash courts. Perfect for families. €€€

Molfetta Beach
Tel: 26610 91915/9
Fax: 26610 91919
www.molfettabeach.com
Situated a stone's throw from the beach in busy little Gouviá, the 28-room Molfetta – modest but good value – is 7km (around 4 miles) from the capital. There's a good in-house restaurant, two bars, a disco – and a Sunday night Greek dancing demonstration. Ask for a room with a sea view. €

Kanóni
Corfu Holiday Palace
Nafsikas Street
Tel: 26610 36540
Fax: 26610 36551/45933
This high-rise, with 256 rooms, 14 suites and 35 bungalows, located on the Kanóni peninsula, has lovely views of Pontikoníssi. The hotel has two pools, a private beach, air-conditioning, health club, tennis, a watersports school, an in-house restaurant and the Kefi Bar – plus the casino, and free transfers to the Corfu Golf Club. Ask for newly renovated rooms with sea views – extensive renovations are underway. Open all year. €€€

Kérkyra (Corfu Town)
Bella Venezia
4 N Zambéli Street
Tel: 26610 46500/44290/20707
Fax: 26610 20708
www.bellaveneziahotel.com
Owned by Mr Theodore Ziniatis, this is a special place. Comprising 30 rooms and one suite, completely renovated in the winter of 2005, in a quiet neoclassical mansion at the south edge of the old town, it has wonderful, personalised service, is open year round, and is convenient for everything. There is air-conditioning and an in-house bar, and you can take breakfast in the garden. €€

Cavalieri
4 Kapodhistriou Street
Tel: 26610 39336
Fax: 26610 39283
www.cavalieri-hotel.com
An A-class hotel occupying a 17th-century building overlooking the Spianádha, the Albanian coast and the Paleó Froúrio. Frankly overpriced, with smallish rooms, but almost all of them have sea views from Venetian balconies, and the roof garden makes the place. Open all year. €€€

Corfu Palace
2 Dhimokratías, north end of Garítsa Bay
Tel: 26610 39485
Fax: 26610 31749
www.corfupalace.com
Kérkyra's town's only 'Lux' class establishment, this enjoys a high level of repeat clientele, including VIPs and foreign dignitaries, especially during May and September. They come for the 115 huge rooms (renovated in 1995) with marble tubs in the baths, the huge seawater pool, the big breakfasts at the generally excellent restaurant and the assiduous level of service. Open all year. €€€

Hotel Arcadion
2 Vlasopoulou Street
Tel: 26610 30104
Fax: 26610 45087
www.arcadionhotel.com
This six-storey, 33-roomed hotel, renovated in bright, faux-neoclassical style in 2003, is the most central in the capital. Upper-storey Spianádha-side rooms have lovely views; avoid rooms directly above the (admittedly rather posh) ground-level McDonald's. €€

Konstantinoupolis
Zavitsianoú 11, Old Port
Tel: 26610 48716
Fax: 26610 48718
This 1862-dated building, the first ever built in town and for long a backpackers' dosshouse, has been lovingly restored in accor-

Left: Nefeli Hotel

dance with its vintage as a well-priced C-class hotel with sea and mountain views. On-site restaurant and heating, though no air conditioning. Open all year. €€

Siorra Vittoria
36 Stefanou Padova Street
Tel: 26610 36300, 69369 99988
E-mail: metaxas@otenet.gr
Named after the owner's Corfiot grandmother, this neoclassical boutique hotel (renovated in 2005) has nine glorious rooms and suites around a lovely garden. The architect and owner, has spared no expense, from flat-screen TVs to *trompe-l'oeil* murals. €€€

Komméno
Grecotel Corfu Imperial
Tel: 26610 91490
Fax: 26610 91881
www.grecotel.gr
This is universally acknowledged as the best hotel on the island – and yet the staff are so personable and friendly that it doesn't have that snobbishness one might expect. The location, on the Komméno Peninsula, 10km (6 miles) from Kérkyra, is exquisite, the hotel is beautifully designed, and the restaurants, bars, shops, fitness club, watersport school, pools and private beaches all make the stiff rates worth it. Three grades of lodging: standard rooms, bungalows and a few super-luxe villas (the latter at around €800). €€€

Grecotel Eva Palace
PO Box 57, Tzavros
Tel: 26610 90003
Fax: 26610 91699/91237
www.grecotel.gr
This 4-star member of the elegant Grecotel chain is another ornament on the stunning Komméno peninsula. With 240 rooms, on-site restaurants, bars, pools and sports facilities, this hotel caters for couples and honeymooners. €€€

Kondókali
Kontokali Bay
Tel: 26610 99000–2
Fax: 26610 91901
www.kontokalibay.com
This hotel/bungalow complex with sea views is on the wooded Kondókali Peninsula, 6km

(4 miles) from the capital. Catering for families, it has elegant public rooms, marble baths, air-conditioning, three restaurants, a pool and two beaches. Superior sea-view rooms in the main building are preferable. €€€

Liapádhes
Liapades Beach
Tel: 26630 41115/41370/26630
Two smallish wings, not monopolised by tour groups, make up this amiable C-class hotel at one of the quieter beach resorts on the west-central coast. One restored old building contains 28 standard rooms; the modern unit has 10 self-catering studios. €€

Nissáki
Falcon Travel
Tel: 26630 91318
Fax: 26630 91070
www.falcon-travel-corfu.com
British-owned travel agency that can arrange stays in either a dozen beach-side apartments in the area or two sensitively restored houses in the idyllic Mt Pandokrátor hamlet of Tritsí. € apartments, €€ village houses.

Paleokastrítsa
Akrotiri Beach
Paleokastrítsa
Tel: 26630 41237/41275/22227
Fax: 26630 41277
www.akrotiri-beach.com
Long a fixture of Paleokastrítsa, this high-rise has 127 rooms, many with incomparable views of the bays. There are two beautiful pools, a restaurant, beach bar, tennis courts, pebbly beach and watersports. Open Apr–Oct. €€

Fundana Villas
4km before Paleokastrítsa
Tel: 26630 22532
A 17th-century Venetian farm-manor that's been converted into a bungalow complex, with the old olive press as the main common area. Good for families (the units hold up to five people), with a pool and 8-ha (20-acre) setting near the north end of the lovely Rópa valley. Ask your host about hikes and walks in the countryside here. Open Mar–Oct. €€

A smallish hotel in neoclassical style taking advantage of this village's famous views over the Ionian and the lush countryside. Swimming pool and good breakfasts make up for a lack of beachside setting. Unusually for a rural hotel, it's open until November. €€

Perouládhes
Villa de Loulia
Tel/Fax: 26630 95394
This tiny (nine rooms/suites) neoclassical jewel is 34km (21 miles) from the capital, less than 500m (¼ mile) from Longás Beach, beyond the Canal d'Amour. The building, dating from 1803, is owned by Ms Loukia Mataranga, and creature comforts – antiques, orthopaedic mattresses, internet service, and flowers and fruit on arrival – abound. €€€

Paxí
Paxi Beach
Gaïos
Tel: 26620 31211
Hillside bungalow complex leading down through trees to its own small pebble beach about 2km (1 mile) east of town. €€

Paxós Club
Gaïos
Tel: 26620 32450
Fax: 26620 32097
www.paxosclub.gr
On the outskirts of Gaïos, 20 minutes' walk from the sea, the Paxós Club comprises 26 attractive studios and apartments circling a pool. €€

Pithari Villas
Gaïos
Tel/Fax: 26620 32491
www.pitharivillas.gr
Only 50m (160ft) from the marina in the port of Gaïos, this accommodation comprises a villa, which sleeps six, apartments for two and four guests, and a cottage for two, all furnished with antiques and surrounded by lush gardens. A wonderful place to stay. €€

Pélekas
Levant
Tel: 26610 94230/94335
Fax: 26610 94115
www.levanthotel.com

Sgómbou
Casa Lucia
Tel: 26610 91419
Fax: 26610 91732
www.casa-lucia-corfu.com
These 10, large, self-contained cottages share gracious public space, a pool and a delightful garden. Open all year and owned by Ms Val Androutsopoulou, the Casa Lucia sponsors New Age courses, classes, retreats and clinics *(see page 52)*. No credit cards. €€

Yialiskári
Yialiskari Palace Hotel
Tel: 26610 54401–2
Fax: 26610 54724
www.hotels-corfu.org
Overlooking Yaliskari Bay, 15km (9 miles) from the capital, this member of the Rizos hotel chain has 230 rooms and suites, pool, tennis courts, sauna, and an in-house restaurant and bar. €€€

HEALTH & EMERGENCIES

Hygiene/General Health
Tap water is safe to drink in the Ionian islands, but bottled water – especially the two Greek sparkling brands, Sariza and Souroti – tastes much better.

Sun and heat stroke, and the ill effects of too much alcohol (or too much olive oil) consumed while on holiday are the most

Above: a police officer ready to assist

common health challenges faced by visitors. However, scooter and motorbike mishaps are also a very real hazard on Corfu: only ride any two-wheeler here if you are a proficient motorcyclist, and always wear protective clothing, strong shoes and a helmet, even though the weather might be stifling. Otherwise, hire a car instead.

Be aware that there are some unfriendly, if rarely encountered, creatures on the island. Poisonous vipers really do want to get out of your way before you tread on them, but on rare occasions they don't, so wear sensible walking boots and watch your step. To protect against sea urchins, swim in purpose-made slippers (and wear goggles or a mask so you can spot them); footwear should also take care of the threat from the bottom-dwelling weever fish *(drákena)*, whose poisonous spines contain a potentially lethal toxin. If precautions fail, try to neutralise the poison by applying uncomfortably hot water to the affected site while waiting for a doctor.

Note: flying within 24 hours of scuba diving can bring on nitrogen embolism, requiring an emergency transfer to a decompression chamber.

Pharmacies
Pharmacies/chemists *(farmakía)* abound on Corfu, but I have two favourites in Kérkyra: Mrs Sylvaine Kavadas Pharmacy, 66 Evgheníou Voulgáreos Street, tel: 26610 25378; and K Grammenandi and N Trivizas Pharmacy/Homeopathics, 76 Evgheníou Voulgáreos Street, tel: 26610 30100.

Medical/Dental Services
Depending on the nature of your dental or health needs, either consult your hotel concierge for a list of accredited and trusted physicians and dentists; phone the Tourist Police; or go by taxi or ambulance to Corfu General Hospital *(Yenikó Nosokomío Kérkyras)*, where the emergency room staff will make a diagnosis.
Corfu General Hospital: Corner Andreadí and Konstandá streets, near San Rocco, tel: 26610 88200.
Medical Bioprognosis SA (private clinic): 19th km Paleokastritsa Road (near Doukádes); tel: 26630 42056/41345.

Emergency Telephone Numbers
Ambulance: tel: 166 or 26610 39403
Fire: tel: 26610 199/191
Police: tel: 100 (see also regional numbers below)
Tourist Police: 4 Samartzí Street, San Rocco Square, Kérkyra; tel: 26610 30265
Traffic Police: tel: 26610 39294
Breakdowns: ELPA, tel: 26610 39504; **Express Service**, tel: 154 or 26610 44244. The local number generally works better.
Regional Police Numbers
Ághios Matthéos, tel: 26610 75113
Argyrádhes, tel: 26620 51422
Benítses, tel: 26610 72222
Gaïos, Paxí, tel: 26620 32222
Karousádhes, tel: 26630 31222
Kastelláni, tel: 26610 54222
Lefkími, tel: 26620 22222
Magouládhes, tel: 26630 95222
Othoní, Dhiapóndia islets, tel: 26630 71592
Paleokastrítsa, tel: 26630 41203
Skriperó, tel: 26630 22222
Yiannádes, tel: 26610 51222
Yimári, tel: 26630 91261
Ýpsos, tel: 26610 93204

COMMUNICATION & NEWS

Postal Services
The main Post Office *(Tahydhromío)* in Kérkyra is located at the corner of Alexándhras Avenue and Rizospáston Vouleftón Street (tel: 26610 25544; Mon–Fri 7.30am–2pm, also some evening hours, check for times). Note: upon entering, be sure to take a number from an automated machine and wait your turn.

Yellow post boxes for ordinary mail are situated all over the island; red boxes are for express mail. Post offices in Greece have specific windows for regular post and stamps *(grammatósima)*, sending parcels, *post restante* and girobank transactions.

Telephones
There are numerous phone boxes across the island, usually stationed at the noisiest intersections, which take OTE (Greek telecom) phone cards; these are available at kiosks *(períptera)*, newsagents and other sorts of shops in several denominations, and are the

cheapest way of making calls. If you're not going to be around long enough to get full use out of a card, seek out the growing number of countertop pay-phones which take 5-, 10- and 20-cent coins, or find one of the few remaining metered phones at a kiosk (where you pay after making the call). However, none of these types of phones can be rung back, which makes it problematic for people to stay in touch with you. The best solution for that is to carry a mobile phone. Almost all European providers have roaming agreements with at least one of the three mobile networks trading in Greece. In any event, avoid using hotel room phones, at least for outgoing calls – the surcharges can run up to four times the basic OTE rate.

To make international calls, dial 00, followed by the country code, the area code (omitting the initial 0 except for Italy) then the number.

Directory Enquiries: tel: 131
International Directory Enquiries: tel: 161.
Internet Access
For listings of internet cafés, see pages 78–9.

Media

Corfu supports a huge number of local newspapers and broadcasting stations, but visitors will probably confine themselves to the major television channels received at their hotels and radio stations picked up in hire cars. Day-later foreign press is readily available across the island (*see pages 70–1* for Kérkyra newsagents).

The Corfiot: Corfu's English Language Monthly Magazine (PO Box 445, tel: 26610 52833; www.corfunews.net) is edited by the local author and leader of walks and excursions *extraordinaire*, Hilary Whitton Païpeti, and is packed with useful information.

USEFUL INFORMATION

Visitors with Disabilities

Greece – and Corfu is no exception – is a challenge for visitors with disabilities. Accommodation, transport, sites, toilets – nothing is truly disabled-friendly, although should change in time due to EU directives. However, Kérkyra itself, readily accessible from the airport by taxi, and not criss-crossed

with flights of steps, is far easier to negotiate than, say, Athens or the Cyclades.

Contact one of the travel agents recommended on page 96 and discuss your special needs with them before planning your trip. They should be able to map out accommodation, excursions and transport to suit.

Children

Young visitors are universally welcomed on the island. Most of the itineraries in this guide have been designed with travellers of all ages and abilities in mind, and all the accommodation has been vetted with an eye to young people's needs. Corfu is much better prepared for families with young children than some of the more sophisticated islands further south, though you may choose not to take youngsters to Kávos, or the nudist beach at Myrtiótissa.

THE GREEK LANGUAGE

Greek is a phonetic language. There are some combinations of vowels and consonants that customarily stand for certain sounds and some slight pronunciation changes determined by which letter follows but, generally, sounds are pronounced as they are written.

Above: views south from Chlomós

P	ρ	r in raisin	ro
Σ	σ	s in sun, except pronounced z before g & m sounds	sigma
T	τ	t in trireme	taf
E	ε	y in clearly	ipsilon
Φ	φ	f in favour	fi
X	χ	h in help	hi
Ψ	ψ	ps in copse	psi
Ω	ω	o in oh	omega

Diphthongs

Type	Value
αι	e in hey
αυ	av or af in avert or after
ει	i in ski
ευ	ev or ef
οι	i in ski
ου	oo in poor

Double consonants

μπ	b at beginnings of words; mb in the middle of words
ντ	d at beginnings of words; nd in the middle of words
τζ	dz as in adze
γγ, γκ	g at the beginnings of words; ng in the middle of words

Vocabulary

Note: The following words are broken into syllables (not separate words), the stressed syllable marked with an accent. Greeks don't accent one-syllable words, but we do for clarity. Pronounce *e* as in pet; *a* as in father; *i* as in ski; *o* as in oh; *u* as in tune.

Numbers

Note: many foods and drinks take the feminine form of 'one' (*mí-a*).

one *é-na* (neuter)/*é-nas* (masc.)/*mí-a* (fem.)
two *dhýo*
three *trí-a* (neuter)/*tris* (masc. and fem.)
four *té-sse-ra, tésseres* (masc. and fem.)
five *pén-de*
six *éxi*
seven *ep-tá/eftá*
eight *ok-tó*
nine *e-né-a/enyá*
ten *dhéka*
eleven *éndheka*
twelve *dhódheka*
thirteen *dhe-ka-trí-a/dhe-ka-trís*

If you touch down in Athens en route to Corfu, you will find that most Athenians have some knowledge of English, and most Greeks are delighted to find a visitor making stabs at speaking Greek. (The Greeks should not ridicule you for making mistakes but may correct you: they themselves have a hard time with Greek spelling and the complex Greek grammar.)

In addition to pronouncing each letter, remember that stress plays a vital role in Modern Greek. Each Greek word has a single main stress (marked in the following vocabulary list with an accent).

Greek is an inflected language and noun and adjective endings change according to gender, number and case. Case endings and the conjugation of Greek verbs are, unfortunately, beyond the scope of a guide book.

The Greek Alphabet

Cap.	l.c.	Value	Name
A	α	a in father	alfa
B	β	v in visa	vita
Γ	γ	ghama, gh when medial, y when initial	
Δ	δ	th in then	delta
E	ε	e in let	epsilon
Z	ζ	z in zebra	zita
H	η	i in ski	ita
Θ	θ	th in theory	thita
I	ι	i in ski	yota
K	κ	k in king	kapa
Λ	λ	l in million	lamda
M	μ	m in mouse	mi
N	ν	n in no	ni
Ξ	ξ	x as in box	ksi
O	ο	o in oh	omikron
Π	π	p in pebble	pi

Above: the way ahead

fourteen *dhe-ka-té-sse-ra/dhékatésseres*
etc. until twenty
twenty *í-ko-si*
thirty *tri-án-da*
forty *sa-rán-da*
fifty *pe-nín-da*
sixty *exínda*
seventy *ev-dho-mín-da*
eighty *og-dhón-da*
ninety *e-ne-nín-da*
one hundred *e-ka-tó*
two hundred *dhi-a-kó-si-a* (neuter)
three hundred *tri-a-kó-si-a* (neuter)
four hundred *te-tra-kó-si-a* (neuter)
one thousand *hí-lia* (neuter)

Note: Since the word for euro *(evró)* is neuter and undeclined, a number preceding it is also neuter. Thus, *téssera evró*, for 4 euros.

Days of the Week
Monday *Def-té-ra*
Tuesday *Trí-ti*
Wednesday *Te-tár-ti*
Thursday *Pém-pti*
Friday *Pa-ras-ke-ví*
Saturday *Sá-vva-to*
Sunday *Ky-ri-a-kí*
yesterday *kthes*
today *sí-me-ra*
tomorrow *á-vri-o*

Greetings
Hello *yiá sas* (plural/polite)/*yiá sou* (sing./familiar) *yiá* (abbreviated)
Good day *ka-li mé-ra*
Good evening *ka-lí spé-ra*
Good night *kalí ník-ta*
Welcome *ka-lós íl-tha-te*
How are you? *Ti ká-ne-te?* (plural/polite)/ *Ti ká-nis?* (singular/familiar)
fine (in response) *ka-lá*
pleased to meet you *há-ri-ka*

Getting Around
yes *né*
no *ó-hi*
okay *en dá-x-i*
thank you *ef-ha-ris-tó*
excuse me *sig-nó-mi*
It doesn't matter *dhen pirázi*
It's nothing *tí-po-ta*
certainly/polite yes *má-li-sta*

Can I..? *Bo-ró na..?*
When? *Pó-te?*
Where is..? *Poú í-n-e..?*
Do you speak English? *Mi-lá-te an-gli-ká?*
Do you understand? *Ka-ta-la-vé-ne-te?*
What time is it? *Ti ó-ra í-ne?*
What time will it leave? *Ti ó-ra tha fýghi?*
I don't *dhén* (plus verb)
I want *thé-lo*
I have *é-ho*
here/there *e-dhó/e-kí*
near/far *kon-dá/ma-kry-á*
small/large *mi-kró/me-gá-lo*
quickly *grí-go-ra*
slowly *ar-gá*
good/bad *ka-ló/ka-kó*
warm/cold *zes-tó/krý-o*
bus *le-o-for-í-o*
boat *ka-rá-vi, va-pó-ri*
hydrofoil *dhelfíni*
scooter *papáki*
motorcycle *motosikléta*
bicycle *podhílato*
ticket *i-si-tí-ri-o*
road/street *dhró-mos/o-dhós*
beach *pa-ra-lí-a*
sea *thá-la-ssa*
church *e-kli-sí-a*
ancient ruin *ar-hé-a*
centre *kén-dro*
square *pla-tí-a*

Hotels
hotel *xe-no-dho-hí-o*
Do you have a room? *É-he-te é-na dho-má-ti-o?*
bed *kre-vá-ti*
shower with hot water *doúz mé zes-tó neró*
key *kli-dhí*
toilet *toua-lé-ta*
women's *yi-ne-kón*
men's *án-dron*

Shopping
store *ma-ga-zí*
kiosk *pe-ríp-te-ro*
open/shut *a-nik-tó/klis-tó*
post office *ta-hy-dhro-mí-o*
stamp *gra-ma-tó-simo*
letter *grám-ma*
envelope *fá-ke-lo*
telephone *ti-lé-fo-no*
bank *trá-pe-za*

marketplace *a-go-rá*
Have you..? *É-he-te..?*
Is there..? *É-hi..?*
How much does it cost? *Pó-so ká-ni?*
It's (too) expensive *Í-ne (po-lý) a-kri-vó*
How many? *Pó-sa?*

Emergencies
doctor *yia-trós*
hospital *no-so-ko-mí-o*
pharmacy *far-ma-kí-o*
police *as-ti-no-mí-a*
station *stath-mós*

USEFUL ADDRESSES

Tourist Offices
EOT, or the Hellenic Tourist Organisation
of Greece (corner of Rizospáston Voulseftón
and Polylá streets, Kérkyra; tel: 26610
37520/37638; Mon–Fri 8am–2pm)

Travel Agencies
Aperghi Travel and Tourism
Dhimokratías Avenue and 1 I Polylá Street
Tel: 26610 48713–14
Fax: 26610 48715
E-mail: aperghi@travelling.gr
www.travelling.gr/aperghi
Ms Anna S Aperghi is a long-time tourism
professional, and her service is personalised,
prompt and cordial. Fax or e-mail to arrange
accommodation. An attractive option is a
7- or 14-day tour based on the Corfu Trail.
Paxós Magic Holidays
Gaïos, Paxós
Tel: 26620 32269
Fax: 26620 32122
www.paxosmagic.com
Managed by Mr Kostas Grammatikos and
family, this agency can arrange all your lodg-
ing, car and other needs on Paxí, Andípaxí,
Corfu and the mainland.

FURTHER READING

A few of these books are now rare, but don't
give up – most can be found at a reasonable
price not only on Amazon (.co.uk and .com),
but also Barnes & Noble (www.bn.com) and
www.abebooks.com. Online, you can also

access *Elizabeth Boleman-Herring's Greece:
The Thinking Traveler's Guide to Hellas*, at
www.greecetraveler.com.
Captain Correlli's Mandolin by Louis de
Bernières (Mandarin/Vintage). Though set
on nearby Kefalloniá, this war-and-romance
epic is a distillation of all things Ionian.
Don't judge it by the truly forgettable 2001
movie starring Nicholas Cage and Penelope
Cruz; it's a complex and occasionally dark
work which caused considerable controversy
in Greece for its less-than-flattering portrayal
of the World War II resistance movement.
Corfu: The Garden Isle, edited by Spiro
Flamburiari and Frank Giles (John Murray,
now o/p). Beautifully illustrated book that's
a native son's labour of informed love.
Edward Lear: The Corfu Years, edited and
introduced by Philip Sherrard (Denise Harvey,
UK & Greece). The late philhellenic scholar
Sherrard produced an engaging portrait of
watercolourist, humourist and 19th-century
Balkan traveller Lear in this welcome reis-
sue; the original is expensive antiquarian stock.
*Ionia Nissia: Sta Ihni tou Odyssea/The
Ionian Islands: In the Tracks of Odysseus.*
Photographs by Nikos Dhessylas, histori-
cal essay (Greek-English) by Nikos
Moskhonas (Synolo Publications, Greece).
Local photographer Dhessylas' stunning
portfolio is an essential souvenir purchase.
*In the Footsteps of Lawrence Durrell and
Gerald Durrell in Corfu (1935–39): A Mod-
ern Guidebook* by Hilary Whitton Païpeti
(Hermes Press, Corfu). Easily available at
island bookshops.
*Prospero's Cell: A Guide to the Landscape
and Manners of the Island of Corcyra* (Faber
& Faber/Marlowe & Co). First penned in 1960
and in print once again, this is a nostalgic sur-
vey of characters and customs from the 1930s.
*Prospero's Kitchen: Mediterranean Cook-
ing of the Ionian Islands from Corfu to
Kythera* (Pedestrian Publications, Corfu &
UK/M Evans & Co). An amalgam of history, local lore and heirloom recipes.
*The Second Book of Corfu Walks: The Road
to Old Corfu (Hermes Press, Corfu)* and *The
Companion Guide to the Corfu Trail* (Pedestrian Productions, Corfu & UK). Detailed
walks across the island by Hilary Whitton
Païpeti; the Corfu Trail is a long-distance
route from one end of the island to the other.

Right: clear waters

ACKNOWLEDGEMENTS

Photography	**Elizabeth Boleman-Herring** *and*
10, 11, 12, 13,	**AKG Photo**
14	**Byzantine Museum**
15	**Topham Picturepoint**
23, 24t&b, 37, 45, 72	**Phil Wood/Apa Publications**
56, 77	**Paul Murphy/Apa Publications**
Cover	**Medioimages/Imagestate**
Cartography	**Berndtson & Berndtson**

The author would like to thank Maria Loumou; Anna Aperghi and Christos Priftis of
Aperghi Travel; Theodore Ziniatis and his staff, Stylian Vlachou, Marilena Louvrou and
Spyros Anthis, of the Bella Venezia; and Vasiliki Katsarou, of the Rex restaurant, whose
walnut pie is reason enough to visit Corfu.

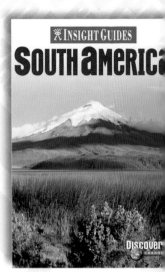

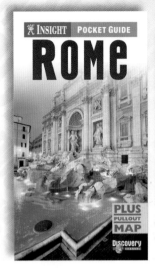
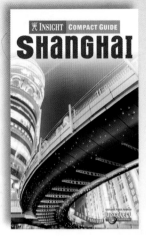

✗ INSIGHT GUIDES

The World Leader in Visual Travel Guides & Maps

As travellers become ever more discriminating, Insight Guides is using the vast experience gained over three-and-a-half decades of guidebook publishing to create an even wider range of titles to serve them. For those who want the big picture, Insight Guides and Insight City Guides provide comprehensive coverage of a destination. Insight Pocket Guides supply personal recommendations for a short stay. Insight Compact Guides are attractively portable. Insight FlexiMaps are both rugged and easy to use. And specialist titles cover shopping, eating out, and museums and galleries. Wherever you're going, our writers and photographers have already been there – more than once.

INDEX

Accommodation 87–90
Achilles 32–34
Adam, Sir Frederick 27
Aegli (restaurant) 27, 34, 73
Ághios Ioánnis Peristerón 64
Ághios Matthéos 48
Ághios Stéfanos Sinión 44, 66
Ághios Stéfanos Avliotón 47
Agnes Restaurant 61
Agní Beach 44
Ahíllion, the 32–34
Akron Beach Bar and Tennis Court 56
Alekos' Beach 30, 73
Alonáki Bay 48–49
alternative therapies 50–51
Andípaxi 43
Angelókastro 54–55
Anglikó Nekrotafío 59
Archaeological Museum of Corfu 23–24
Ariás Beach 66
Art Café and Bar 29, 76
Art Galleries 69

Bandstand (Pálko) 25
Benítses 64
bistros 76
bouzoúki/bouzoúkia 77, 78, 79
British Cemetery 59
British Protectorate 15, 25–27
business hours 86
Byzantine Collection of Corfu 25
Byzantine Museum 31
Byzantium 13

Café Yiali 41
caïques 45–47, 65–67
Campiello Quarter, Kérkyra 39–42
Canal d'Amour 46–47
Casa Lucia 50–51
casino 77
Cathedral (Greek Orthodox) 41
Cathedral (Roman Catholic) 58
Catholicism 14, 58
Chapel of Ághios Arsénios 66
children 93
Christianity 13–14
Church of Ághios Andónios 40

Church and Monastery of Panaghía Vlahernón 35–37, 63
Church of St Francis 40
Church of St George of the Old Fortress 26
Church of St John the Baptist 39
Church of the Archangels 64
Church of Panaghía Tenédhou 31
Church of the Miracleworking St Spyrídhon 16, 28
Church of the Pandokrátor 37
Church of Panaghía Andivouniótiossa 31
Church of Panaghía Mandhrakíou 27
Church of Panaghía ton Xénon 39
Climate box 84
colonisers 11
Constantinople 13
Corcyra 11–12
Corfiot School of Fine Arts 30
Corfu Golf Club 62, 95
Corinthians 11–12
credit cards 85
cricket 15, 95
Customs 84

Dhassiá 32, 34
Dhiapóndia islets 46
disabled visitors 92
Duomo 58
Durrell, Lawrence 16, 39, 66

Elisabeth, Empress of Austria 32–34
Elm Tree Taverna 38
emergency phone numbers 91
Eríkoussa 46–47
Érmones Beach 63
Eucalyptus//Evkalypros (restaurant) 44

Family Taverna 49
Festivals/processions 16, 80–81
flora 38, 59
Folklore Museum of Central Corfu 56–57
food 72–76
further reading 96

Gaïos 42–43
Gardíki 48
Garítsa Bay 28
George I 15

index

getting around 86
getting to Corfu 83
ginger beer 28
Glyfádha Beach 61
golf 62
Grecotel Corfu Imperial 57–58
Greek dancing 57
Greek phrases 94–95

Halikoúnas Beach 49
health 90–91
history 11–17
Hlomós 64
Holy Trinity Anglican Church 58
Homer 11
horse-riding 62
Hotel Erikoússa 47
hotels 87–90
hydrofoils 42, 83

Icons 31, 37, 38, 39
Il Pareo (shop) 43
internet cafés 78, 79

Jewellery 70–71

Kafeneion Kanóni 37
Kaiser Wilhelm II's Bridge 64
Kaiser's Throne 63
Kalámi 66
Kanóni 35, 37
Kapodhístrias, John 15, 25, 41
Kávos 65
Kerasiá 44
Kérkyra (town) 23–32, 58–60
Kochíli Restaurant 44
Kommoteírio Salon 51
Kouloúra 66
kumquat/kumquat products 39, 69

La Famiglia (restaurant) 28, 54, 74
La Lucciola Taverna 51
La Rosa di Paxós (restaurant) 43
Lake Korissíon 49
Lákka 43
Lákones 55
language 93–95
Lemoniá 40
liqueurs 39, 69, 70

Listón, the 27
Longós 43

Maitland, Thomas 15, 25
Medi Jeunesse 51
media 92
Menigos Beach Resort 61
Mitrópoli 40
Ministry of Culture Museum Shop 25
Myrtiótissa (nudist beach) 52–53
Mon Repos 28
Monastery of the Holy Virgin 55–56
Monastery of Pandokrátoros Ypsiloú 38
money 85
Mount Pandokrátor 38
Mourághia 40
Mouse Island 35
Mulberry Tree (restaurant) 54
Municipal Art Gallery 29–30
Museum of Asian Art 27

Nautilus Café 28
New Fortress 31–32
New Fortress's Morrison Café 58
nightlife 77–79
Nikifórou Theotóki Street, Kérkyra 39
Normans 13
nudist beaches 52–53

O Yiannis (taverna) 29
OCC Yachting 67
Odysseus 11
Odyssey 11
Old Fortress Café 26, 76
Old Fortress 25–26
Old Port 41
olive wood crafts 38, 43, 69
orchids 59
Orthodoxy 14, 40
Ottoman Turks/Empire 14–15, 16, 27

Palace of St Michael and St George 27
Paleokastrítsa 11, 55–56
Papayeorghis Shop 39
Paxí 42–43
Pélekas 63
Pithari Villas 43
Platía Yeorghíou Theotóki 39
Pondikoníssi 35, 37

port authorities 83
postal service 91
Professional Diving Center 67
Psaïlas, George 59
public holidays 87

Religion 85
restaurants *(see also individual entries)*
   72–76
Rex (restaurant) 23, 27, 34
Romans 13
Rópa Valley Stables 62
Rópa Valley 62
Rotunda 25

Safety 85
St Spyrídhon 16, 28, 80, 81
San Rocco Square, Kérkyra 60
Schulenberg, Field Marshal Johann
   Matthias von der 14–27
scuba diving 67
Serbian cemetery 26
Sgómbou 50
shopping 69–71
Sidhári 46
Silvereyes (shop) 43
Sinarádhes 56–57
snakes 91
Soueref, Vana 51
Spiliá Gate 31, 40
Spianádha 13, 25

sport 95
Square of Kremastí 41
Strinýlas 38
Summer Cinema Phoenix 60
synagogue (Scuola Greca) 40

Taverna Agni 44
Taverna Galíni 66
telephones 92
Temple of Artemis 24
Toula (restaurant) 45
tourist information offices 95
transport 83, 86
travel agencies 95–96
tsitsibýra 28

Vaccinations 84
Venetian Walls 41
Venetian Well (restaurant) 41, 75
Venetians/Venice 13–15, 25, 31
Vídhos islet 32
visas/passports 84
Vivi (caïque) 65–67
Vlahérna islet 35

White House 66
Whitton Païpeti, Hilary 58, 59, 92
Wilhelm II, Kaiser 33–34, 63
Winter Cinema Orfeas 60

Yachting 67